FRENCH COOKING IS THE MOST APPETIZING
AND ECONOMICAL WAY OF SERVING DELICIOUS,
SATISFYING, MAGNIFICENT MEALS!

This is the basic book for cooks who want to produce the
celebrated dishes of France in their own kitchens the
way a French housewife would prepare them for her own
family. All of the recipes have been adapted to American
methods and use ingredients easily found in the super-
market.

Fernande Garvin was born and educated in France. She
learned to love good food and good cooking at her
family's table. With typical French flair for hearty but
exquisite dishes, and sensible but practical economy,
she tells you how to feed your friends and relations in
grand style—but simply, easily and cheaply.

THE ART OF FRENCH COOKING

The Art of French Cooking

Fernande Garvin

BANTAM BOOKS
TORONTO · NEW YORK · LONDON

THE ART OF FRENCH COOKING

A Bantam Book / published September 1958

2nd printing .... April 1959	3rd printing ... September 1960
4th printing .... February 1961	
Bantam Reference Library edition published March 1962	
6th printing ... September 1962	7th printing .... June 1963
8th printing .... March 1964	
Bantam Cookbook Shelf edition published July 1965	
10th printing .. September 1965	18th printing .... January 1970
11th printing .... October 1966	19th printing .... June 1970
12th printing ..... March 1967	20th printing .... June 1970
13th printing .... October 1967	21st printing .... August 1970
14th printing .... May 1968	22nd printing .. December 1970
15th printing .... July 1968	23rd printing .... May 1971
16th printing .... July 1969	24th printing .... January 1972
17th printing .... October 1969	25th printing ..... April 1972
26th printing .... June 1972	

27th printing

28th printing

29th printing

Library of Congress Catalog Card Number: 58-9790

Bantam Books are published by Bantam Books, Inc., a National General company. Its trade-mark, consisting of the words "Bantam Books" and the portrayal of a bantam, is registered in the United States Patent Office and in other countries. Marca Registrada. Bantam Books, Inc., 666 Fifth Avenue, New York, N.Y. 10019.

PRINTED IN THE UNITED STATES OF AMERICA

Table of Contents

Chapter I

On Cooking, Eating, and Wine

Fᴇᴇɴᴄʜ "cuisine bourgeoise" is the beloved mother of "grande cuisine." I have not yet met a great chef who did not tell me that he had first learned at home the enjoyment of fine cooking and good eating. But "grande cuisine" is one of those genius offsprings who soar so high from the nest that the mother who has taught them how to fly is filled with a pride mixed with awe.

"Grande cuisine" has become international, and even French families very seldom, or never, eat at home such dishes as "pressed duck" or "tournedos Rossini." For the foreign tourist in France, it is a wonderful surprise to stop at the small country inn or the "restaurant de quartier" and be served a regal meal made with relatively inexpensive ingredients. No truffles, no foie gras, but simple foods cooked with what seems to be an intuitive knowledge of the way each ingredient will react when combined with the others.

1

Another surprise is in store for the foreigner. "I can't understand it," I was told by many Americans. "When you go to a restaurant, you always see the French people at the next table cleaning up dish after dish of the richest food, washing it down with glasses of wine, and polishing off the meal with a snifter of cognac. And, then, you meet them in the stores, in the streets, you look at them: here they are, most of them alert and slim, without a care in their minds or one extra pound on their waist lines. How do they do it?"

I think the answer is that French meals are satisfying and not fattening because of the French way of cooking. French cooking, be it "grande cuisine" or family cooking, is based on one principle:

"Eating is a civilized pleasure. Under normal conditions man does not have any nutrition problem if he eats what he likes. He can forget about eating for subsistence and should look at food as a source of enjoyment."

From this concept spring the characteristic ways of cooking in France.

A Perfect Dish Is like a Melody . . .

There is a French saying, "L'exces en tout est defaut" (Excess is always a fault), which best describes the French way of cooking.

A dish is a blend of different ingredients which either set off or tone down each other in order to create a new and delicious taste. Pungent and aromatic foods are most of the time used very sparingly, though sometimes more freely, but they are always measured to insure the balance of flavors of the finished dish. When a French cook uses cream, or wine, or brandy, or herbs, it is not because they are tasty but because they bring out the flavor of meat or fish, for instance, and become themselves more delicate and different in cooking.

So, the first rule of French cooking is: not too much of

anything. If the flavor of one of the ingredients stands out, the dish is a failure. A French cook follows the traditional recipe exactly, and changes the measurements very gradually and only after tasting.

This respect for the right balance does not kill creativeness, but on the contrary it stimulates the ambition to realize new combinations. Keeping always in mind the fact that a good recipe cannot be improved by increasing the quantity or the number of the ingredients, French cooks achieve a wonderful success by changing the ingredients themselves, thus creating new combinations. This certainly is much more rewarding than to dispense freely oregano and basil and tarragon and, for good measure, chervil and parsley because the cook likes herbs.

"Pour Fat off Skillet" . . .

Foods are cooked in fat for two principal purposes: either to seal the juice in or to cook dry without burning.

There is enough and much more digestible fat in fresh butter, cheese, milk, and cream to make cooking fat quite unnecessary in a normal diet.

Shortening allowed to remain in the finished dish is responsible for most of bad cooking and excess weight.

Plenty of shortening is needed to get good results, but it has no taste value. It is unappetizing and hard to digest. Therefore, whenever the recipe says, "Pour fat off skillet," the French housewife dutifully pours it off. She is not losing much, only extra heaviness. Her cooking and her own weight are that much lighter.

Getting rid of the fat makes it easy for her to "deglacer" the pan. This means that, after cooking, she pours a little hot water, or consommé, or wine, and scrapes loose the brown parts stuck to the bottom of the pan. These brown parts are in a way a concentrate of the juice and, when dissolved in a small volume of liquid, they add much to the flavor and the finesse of the dish.

The Care and Feeding of Body and Soul

A meal in France is a complete production: hors-d'oeuvre variés, a light course of fish, a hearty course of meat and vegetable, a salad, a tray of cheeses with bread and butter, fruit or a sweet dessert, the whole repast preceded by an "aperitif," accompanied by one or two wines, and followed by a brandy or a cordial.

After such a lunch, a Frenchman is peaceful and happy, and goes back to the office where he handles his business with all the alertness and energy of a healthy businessman. After dinner, he will not fall asleep in a chair, at the movies, or at the theatre, and if he has guests the conversation will be animated and as brilliant as it could ever be.

. . . And, on the average, the French stay slim.

Besides the fact that French dishes do not contain as much fat as it seems, there is an all-important reason why French meals are not conducive to overweight: they are fully satisfying.

When you see French people in restaurants, you see them at mealtime—what you may not realize is that mealtime is the *only* time they eat.

French "petit dejeuner"—breakfast—is for most people a cup of coffee or tea; for the others it is coffee with a brioche or a croissant, or a piece of buttered toast with jam. "Café au lait," the delicious coffee with milk of the French breakfast, contains little milk (never cream). There is no second breakfast at the office, no "coffee break" in the morning. Laborers and peasants eat heavy breakfasts and a snack in the morning but, obviously, they need more energy.

After lunch, the next intake of food will be at dinner, and after dinner, nothing more until breakfast. If you have guests during the evening, you offer them coffee (black, because except for the breakfast café au lait, after- and between-meals coffee is always served black, in small cups) or a glass of liqueur. There are no dishes of nuts or candies scattered around for nibbling.

The French do have late supper sometimes, but then they did not have any dinner or they had just a bite to tame their hunger. After the movie or the theater, they will go for a meal to a restaurant where they will again be under the scrutiny of the tourists, aghast at seeing them eat a meal at that hour.

What surprises the French tourist in the United States is, "The meals are so light that you leave the table still hungry—but then, Americans never stop eating all day long."

And, of course, in France, milk is for infants, and a glass of milk with the meal is inconceivable—except to a much publicized former French premier.

If French meals fully satisfy hunger until it is time for the next meal, they also have a beneficial psychological effect. It is a well-known fact that overeating springs from a sort of psychological hunger. A feeling of being thwarted, or frustrated, creates a craving for food as a substitute. Naturally, the feeling of not being loved, of not being taken care of, or of being denied gratification is at the root of the same impulse. A French poetess has said, "Les travaux du menage sont une oeuvre d'amour": "The keeping of a home is a labor of love." Elaborate cooking is never worth the trouble for oneself. You cook for others.

One of the first signs of a marriage going to the rocks is the wife's lack of interest in the preparation and serving of the meals. "It's good enough for him" is implied in a neglectful approach to cooking.

Fine, plentiful meals and good wines carry with them the conviction that one is loved and wanted. This sense of full psychological gratification renders unnecessary the "rewarding" of the ego by constant nibbling.

As for the cook herself, she, like the rest of the family, enjoys a delicious meal—and her ego is supported by pride in her achievement and self-esteem for her generosity in devoting time, effort, and talent to the family's happiness.

Of course, French women are not the only ones to bring love and thought to the cooking of the family meals. In every country in the world most wives and mothers do their best to make the meals one of the most cherished experiences. The saying, "There is no cooking like mother's cooking," is a permanent testimony to women's housekeeping qualities in this country.

If cooking seems to play a greater role in France, perhaps it is due not so much to mother, but principally to father. Frenchmen take the time to eat, they never fail to comment on the food, they are lavish with their congratulations, and when they criticize, it is always very much to the point. They think highly of a good cook and let it be known. Beauty, charm, "chic," culture, and brains, in a woman, find enthusiastic admirers in France (as everywhere else), but not more than perfect cooking. To be a good cook is not a greater—but definitely not a lesser—quality than to dress well or to be a brilliant conversationalist. This is because cooking in France is considered one of the major arts.

Cooking as an Art

If the French consider cooking an art and insist that eating well is a mark of civilization, it is not because materialistic pleasures are given too much importance. On the contrary, it is because they seem unimportant in themselves if they are not raised to the level of an artistic achievement.

Hunger is the one essential instinct of man, and in order to survive we have to eat a few times a day, every day of our life. Time, thought, and energy have to be spent in the pursuit and the preparation of food. To make it more efficient, the preparation of food has to be made for a whole group, and has to be consumed by this same group at the same time.

At mealtime, the whole group (basically, the family)

is therefore gathered around the table. Eating leaves the mind free and it is the time when conversation should flow; when ideas, impressions, experiences should be exchanged. More family quarrels or reconciliations have been made around a table than anywhere else, and so much money has been spent on business luncheons that it has become a career to be a "good contact man" and take people to lunch, or dinner, or for "a drink."

There is no hospitality without the offering of food and drink, and refusal to partake of the offering was, in the past, considered a stand against friendship with the host. Even now, a guest who will not accept anything, if he were not to excuse himself on doctor's orders, would create a feeling of uneasiness. To partake of bread and salt, or bread and wine, has always been the bond which sealed the peace pact between host and guest, or two reconciled enemies.

Since food is of such primordial importance in the life of society, it cannot be regarded as simply a necessary means of survival. Civilized man ennobles his instinctive needs by transforming them into esthetic pleasures: we do not wear clothes or build houses only as a shelter against inclement weather; we do not take bubble baths to protect our skin against infections resulting from uncleanliness; we do not marry as soon as we reach puberty with any healthy member of the opposite sex so as to beget children. We marry and have children because we fall in love, and we satisfy hunger because we enjoy eating.

Since cooking is an art, the French approach eating with the same attitude as they would a painting or a concert: it should principally satisfy the sense involved. Smell is nearly as important as taste because of the communication between the palate and the nose and the reaction of one sense to the impression received by the other. Sight is important only in that it should not be offended and disturbed by an unpleasant sensation.

Writing on architecture, Pascal, the famous French philosopher, said: "What is only for the sight is worthless." What in a dish is only for the sight is also worthless, and sometimes ridiculous, or even harmful to the perfection of the dish. To choose a vegetable because of the "color ensemble" of the meal is like adding curlicues to the well-designed frame of a beautiful painting; it is not only painfully "cute," it destroys the perfect balance of the work.

The most popular of all French meals is "bifteck aux pommes"—a steak with French-fried potatoes—and a salad, followed by a tray of cheese. No Frenchman would dream of adding peas or tomatoes or anything else to the meal for a "color effect." The only necessary qualities in the presentation of food are tidiness and order. Neatly sliced meat, carefully arranged vegetables, attractive serving dishes, lovely tableware (peasant earthenware as well as high-priced Limoges is famous), sparkling glassware . . . and good cooking—these are all a Frenchman requires to satisfy his "gourmet" needs. Everything on the table—cloth, tableware, flowers—are the discreet attendants to the king: a perfect meal.

How to Make French Dishes in the U.S.A.

Some French dishes are simply impossible to make in this country because some indispensable ingredients are not available at all (such as what in France is called "cream"), and others are available in only a few stores in some cities (such as shallots).

However, most of the ingredients, or perfectly acceptable replacements, can be easily found in the United States and most French dishes can be made here. Many are already well known and have been integrated into American "cuisine." Others might be added to bring the variety that is so much part of the enjoyment of eating.

No special kitchenware is needed for cooking "French style." Unusual casseroles or earthenware dishes are not necessary—they are not used even in France any more—except, as they are in this country, for a more appealing presentation. French cooks use cast iron, stainless steel, aluminum, copper, and enamel pans as Americans do. All the talk about earthenware cookery, for example, does not make sense at all any more since the advent of gas and electric ranges. Of course you do need special equipment if you intend to cook dishes like "pressed duck," but even if you can afford to buy the press, you would be better off in doing "as the French do" and go to a first-class restaurant which will serve you a heavenly "pressed duck" and offer you, to drink with it, a choice of rare wines.

If you simply intend to make a delicious French meal, all you need is average skill, common ingredients, and standard kitchenware.

Cooking with Wine

"Will you tell us about cooking with wine?" or "You should write a book on cooking with wine." . . . There was a time when, at such remarks, I just looked uncomprehending and asked: "What do you mean by 'cooking with wine'?"

Since then, I have learned my way out of such inquiries without so much as batting an eyelash. I enlarge on a few principles, and if everyone is not completely satisfied, no one has ever said so.

Writing on French cooking, I never thought I would once more have to go through the same routine. Then my publisher told me: "You can't write about wine and about cooking without writing about 'cooking with wine.' You have to add a chapter on it." So here it is.

There is no such thing as "cooking with wine." There are recipes using wine, but the whole idea that there is a "cuisine" based on the use of wine, and rules by which you can cook practically anything with wine, is as surprising as if one said, "cooking with onions" or "cooking with parsley."

Wine is one of the ingredients, no less and no more so than onions, garlic, parsley, bay leaf, or thyme. It is used when it rounds out the general flavor or adds to the mellowness and savor of the whole dish. Wine in cooking loses its alcohol and its taste changes. It is no longer the same product one gets in drinking wine. To add wine to any recipe just for the idea of it, or under the delusion that the final dish will be more refined and "sophisticated" is a lazy and inefficient way of cooking. The delusion shared by many that you can open a can, add two tablespoons of sherry, or brandy, or wine, and make a splendid dish is as destructive of good cooking as the generally shared misconception that a haphazard "potpourri" of spices will give class and character to a meal.

Of course, you may follow your fancy, or your feeling, or your "intuition" or anything you want to call it, but do so with the full knowledge that the use of wine (or spices and herbs, for that matter) is never a short cut to good cooking.

What should be considered when using wine for cooking is how its flavor will blend with the flavors of the other ingredients or set them off. If wine is not part of the recipe, there is no rule you can follow on when and how much you may add. It is up to you to know to what extent you may trust your imagination and creativeness.

A few remarks about wine in cooking:

Most cookbooks tell you never to boil a wine sauce, but each recipe instructs: "bring to boil." The truth of the matter is that a wine sauce (made with table wine; fortified wines are different) should always be allowed to boil in order for the alcohol to evaporate. For the same reason, never cover the pan before all alcohol has evaporated. You may know when it is done just by sniffing the contents of the pan. If you still smell alcohol, continue cooking until you do not smell it any more.

Meat cooked in wine has to be well browned before

the addition of wine, otherwise the meat will be soaked in wine and will not be good.

A few slices of carrots take off the tartness of red wine. All wine sauces are good when reheated.

Wine goes beautifully with herbs and spices—but you definitely can have too much of a good thing.

Wine is like all other ingredients: the better the wine, the better the dish. It would be wasteful to use the greatest wines in cooking, but any wine which is not good for drinking is not good for cooking.

There is no such rule as "white wine with white meat, red wine with red meat," either for drinking or for cooking. Red meat is delicious with white wine (as in "beef à la mode") and red wine with fish (as in "trout in wine") although most of the time fish is cooked with white wine, usually dry—less often with sweet.

French cooks, when they wish to cook creatively with wine, begin by following the proven recipes, and only when they are thoroughly familiar with the use of wine do they try novel ways and new combinations.

A Meal without Wine . . .

> A meal without wine is like
> a day without sunshine.
> BRILLAT-SAVARIN

In France, there is no meal without wine. Depending on the family budget and the occasion, the wine served is "vin ordinaire," or "appellation contrôlée," or "great wine"—but always wine.

In restaurants, in the simplest as in the "plushiest," the question is: "What wine will you have? Red or white?" If you were to answer: "No wine," you would instantly lose the interest of the waiter because he would feel that good food will be wasted on you.

It is a fact that wine enhances the flavor of the food.

The lingering aroma creates a background which sets off the taste of the dish. Wine makes a symphony of a good meal. Between drinking water and drinking wine with the meal, there is the same difference as between hearing a melody played with one hand on the piano and listening to it played by a full orchestra. The greater the wine, the more harmoniously the tune sings and the deeper your enjoyment.

Wine contains a very small percentage of alcohol. The low alcoholic content is just enough to create a feeling of well-being and to stimulate conviviality.

Wine also is rich in minerals and vitamins and—contrary to the general misconception—it is not fattening. An average glass (½ cup) contains 66 calories—less than most fruit juices.

Different Kinds of Wines

In France, "wine" means table wine. Wines fortified with alcohol, as port, sherry, madeira, etc., are considered "aperitifs," although it is acceptable to serve a small glass just after the soup. Champagne may be served with the entire meal, but it is more often a "celebration drink" which does not have to be accompanied by any food. It is the traditional beverage for weddings, anniversaries, nightclub entertaining, etc.

Sparkling Burgundy is practically unknown in France and does not seem to appeal to French taste.

Table wines are red, rosé, or white.

Red wine is made from red grapes fermented with the skin, which contains the pigments (or color). Rosé is made from the same grapes but then the juice is fermented alone, the skin being removed at once. White wine is made either from red grapes growing in cold climate where they cannot reach a complete degree of ripeness or, of course, from green grapes.

There is no French red table wine that is sweet. White wines run the whole gamut from extreme dryness (such as Chablis) to extreme sweetness (Bordeaux Sauternes).

Much confusion exists on the meaning of dryness. For many people, it implies a criticism, because they mistakenly identify the degree of dryness with tartness, acidity, or the degree of alcohol. To some people, a "dry" wine means a strongly alcoholic wine. This is not so. Dry means only "not sweet." Most of the Bordeaux Sauternes, the sweetest of all the naturally sweet wines in the world, have a higher alcoholic content than the dry and very dry white wines of Bordeaux or Burgundy. Therefore, "dry" or "sweet" is neither a fault nor a recommendation in itself. It is one of the characteristics of a particular wine and is to be expected from that wine. A dry Sauternes would be only a poor Sauternes, and there would definitely be something wrong with a sweet Chablis.

American wines are made differently from the French wines and their names may be very confusing because they do not necessarily have the same characteristics as the wines from the French regions from which they have borrowed their names. An American Sauterne, Chablis, or Burgundy has its own quality—very disappointing when you expect a taste conforming to the geographical name; very pleasing when you take it for what it is: a different kind of wine.

What to Know about Wine

All delightful wines are not great wines. Most of them are simply "good" wines, and all the rules which apply to the rare and expensive great wines do not apply to them.

Let's forget for a while the famous Burgundies and the first-growth Chateau-bottled Bordeaux. Nobody, anywhere, drinks them every day. They are the glorious "special occasion" wines and deserve to be handled with all the care (and even the fuss) which unfortunately is associated in this country with the serving and drinking of all wines.

A "good" wine (as opposed to a great one) does not need to rest for days after the shortest transportation. You may very well pick up a bottle at the liquor store for your dinner the same day. Only wine showing signs of sediment (usually greater wines) need resting for the sediment to fall back to the bottom of the bottle.

Not all red wines have to be served at "room temperature," and, anyway, "room temperature" is *not* the temperature of the dining room or the living room. It is cooler and is approximately 55° to 60° F. Furthermore, ordinary good red wine is better when cool, although of course not chilled.

Rosé and white wines should be slightly chilled, but not too much. Letting the bottle stand for an hour in the refrigerator brings it to the right temperature. In a word, avoid extremes; don't warm red wine and don't freeze rosé or white wine.

Which Wine to Serve?

No French person would hesitate on how to answer the question of which wine to serve with which food. The answer is: "A good wine." A good wine is always good, and which one should be selected is entirely a question of personal taste.

People talk of ideal "marriages" of wine and food. It seems to me that the use of the word "marriage" (which is very appropriate) provides the clue.

There is not one woman in the world who would be the ideal mate to every one of the men. We never quite understand other people's love, and how often do we hear: "What does he see in her?" A couple may seem to their acquaintances to be very badly matched—and in spite of it their marriage may be "made in heaven."

The same is true of wine and food. If a would-be "connoisseur" announces that you are guilty of heresy because you drink a white wine with your steak or a light red wine with your fish, let him confine himself within his own narrow limits—and "à votre santé."

However, in beginning your experiments and until you do know what you prefer—or when you have guests whose own preferences you don't know, it is safer to stick to the traditional "matchings."

In short, you can't go wrong if you serve:

With fish and shellfish: a dry, or medium dry, or even sweet white wine.

With poultry: or white meat: a dry white wine or a light red wine.

With red meat: a red wine.

With cheese: (except bland cheeses, such as cream cheese) : a red or a dry white wine.

With a sweet dessert or fruit: a sweet white wine.

Rosé wine and champagne may be served with all kinds of foods.

French Wines

We list only a few of the moderately priced wines.* Great wines are listed in all books on wines.

WHITE

DRY   *Bordeaux:* All the "Graves"
        Burgundy: Chablis, Pouilly-Fuissé,
        white Mâcon
        Côtes du Rhône: White Hermitage
        Alsace: Riesling, Traminer, Sylvaner

* This list is by no means all-inclusive. It is an extremely brief enumeration of some of the moderately priced French wines available everywhere in the U.S.A.

SWEET   *Bordeaux:* Sauternes
         Alsace: Gewürztraminer

RED

Bordeaux: Most regionals are excellent:
"Monopole," Médoc, St. Emilion, Po-
merol, and red Graves.
Burgundy: Beaujolais, red Mâcon
Côtes du Rhône: Red Hermitage

ROSÉ

Bordeaux: Bordeaux rosé
Burgundy: Burgundy rosé
Côtes du Rhône: Tavel
Loire Valley: Rosé d'Anjou
Côtes de Provence: a few good rosés mod-
erately priced. The inexpensive ones
are not worth the money.
As a general rule, rosés are never very
great wines, but some are delightful.
However, it is even truer of rosés than of
other wines: the cheap ones are "cheap."
A good rosé should not be expensive, but
it cannot be inexpensive.

How to Buy French Wines

It is odd that Americans who are so brand-conscious
are at a loss when it comes to buying wine.

Wine is a commodity like all others. You can find wonderful bargains if you buy some little-known brand, but
you also can be making a costly mistake.

The brand names of wines are the name of the shipper
and the name of the importer.

How do you know who are the reliable shippers? Make
a note of the shipper's name (which is always printed on
the label) every time you buy a bottle. If you like the
wine, look for the name of the same shipper when you
buy another wine. After three or four such experiments,

you will know that you can rely on this shipper, whether the wine is a Bordeaux, a Burgundy, or any other.

For Bordeaux wine, the Bordeaux wine shipper's association (ADEB) has set up a committee of experts who actually taste-test the wine submitted for export to the U. S. If the wine meets the high standards of those tests, it is awarded the ADEB seal of quality, which is a small shield, black and gold, affixed to the neck of the bottle.

Domestic Wines

There are no very great domestic wines, comparable to the great Bordeaux Chateaux or the exceptional Burgundies, but there are excellent wines made in the United States.

Here again, buy by brand name and do not try to find bargains. Good domestic wine is not inexpensive.

WHITE

DRY Pinot Blanc
   Sauvignon Blanc
   Pinot Chardonnay
   Riesling
   Traminer
   Chablis
   Sauterne
SWEET Sweet Sauterne
   Sweet Semillon

RED

Claret
Burgundy
Cabernet
Pinot Noir

ROSÉ

Grenache

One word of caution: a domestic "Sauterne" does not have any of the characteristics of the Bordeaux Sauternes (by the way, the American Sauterne is spelled without an "s" at the end) and it can be quite dry, whereas the Bordeaux Sauternes is very sweet. Generally speaking, domestic wines bearing names of French regions (Sauterne, Burgundy, Chablis, etc.) are different from the French ones. Do not go by their name, go by their variety.

Vintages

When it comes to wine, one of the first questions asked of French people is: "What is the best vintage for French wines (or Burgundy, or Bordeaux) ?"

It is a source of never-ending astonishment to the French to realize how much Americans are vintage-conscious.

To the question: "What is the best vintage?" or "Is such year a good vintage year?" the only answer is that there is no answer.

The quality of the wine, besides depending on permanent factors for each vineyard, such as soil, type of vines, etc., is made by the weather. Too much rain, or rain at the wrong time; too little sun when sun is needed, may spoil the quality of the wine produced in a given year. On the other hand, the right combination of rain and sun may encourage the production of perfectly good wine in some indifferent vineyards. Also, of course, there is the skill, experience, and integrity of the wine producer and shipper.

Therefore, if 1945, for instance, is recognized as a great vintage, it means that most of the wine produced in 1945 is good, but what of the specific wine you are purchasing? It may be sunny in the city when it is raining in the suburbs. The wine you are buying may come from a vineyard or a region which has suffered when the rest of France has enjoyed gorgeous weather.

Naturally, the reverse is also true, and some perfect wine may be produced in disastrous vintage years.

Even more important to remember is the fact that wine is living. It has a birth, a youth, a maturity, an old age, and a death. Like human beings, it is sometimes interesting when young, really at its best in maturity, and declining in its old age.*

Going back to our example of 1945, was the 1945 wine great in 1950? Will it be great in the year 2000? If you buy 1945 red wine (and pay the price for a great vintage) in 1958, you are wasting good money and good wine, because the 1945 red wine is not completely mature and, therefore, not yet at its peak. Anyway, you won't buy 1945 because there is practically none left. It has already been drunk (too young) by the people who swear by vintages and who have paid top price for a promise of greatness that was prevented from ever being fulfilled.

Great vintage wine means wine which matures slowly. Lesser wine matures more quickly. Wine can be compared to a beautiful woman: a girl who is destined to be a great beauty is only a pretty girl when she is still a child. An adolescent girl may be strikingly attractive at fifteen or eighteen and become plain at twenty-five, whereas another awkward and ungainly teen-ager turns out to be a beauty only after she has passed adolescence.

1945, 1948, 1949, for instance, still lack complete pulchritude. Meanwhile, 1946, 1947, and even 1951 and 1952 are now perfect.

How would you know? This is where the French are wiser: they know that they cannot know. Only top trade people (wine growers, shippers, importers, competent retailers) who have tasted and continue tasting the wine they handle have an intelligent opinion. Therefore, the only rule to follow is the same that applies to all aspects

* "A fine wine is a living being. Like a young girl, to really know her, you have to watch her blossoming into womanhood in all her charm and beauty." Edouard Kressmann, *La Belle Historie de Mademoiselle de la Vinerie.* (Translated by the author.)

of wine purchasing: rely on the shipper or the importer. Good wine merchants do not sell bad wine.

How to Drink Wine

In plays and movies, when the action calls for a Frenchman drinking wine in a restaurant, it is always good for a laugh to show him sternly looking at the wine the "sommelier" has poured for him to taste; then slowly swirling his glass; deeply sniffing the wine; and tasting it with furrowed brows; then swallowing and beaming his appreciation to the relief of the anxiety-ridden "sommelier."

Well, of course, things are not really like that, but when the French drink an exceptionally good wine or when they wish to measure exactly the quality of a certain one, they do look, swirl, sniff, and taste the wine. For lesser wine, they just inconspicuously sniff it and quickly taste it before swallowing.

You don't have to go through the whole ceremony each time you drink wine, but why should you deny yourself the full enjoyment of the good things in life? And wine is definitely one of them.

Wine is better when the bottle has been opened an hour before the meal, and when the glass is only half-filled. This is because as soon as it comes in contact with air, wine begins to breathe and the oxygen develops the full strength of the "bouquet." Therefore, since the glass is to be only half filled and room is to be left for all the fragrance to expand, it is preferable to use a large, orange-shaped glass.

The wine is swirled in the glass to intensify the oxygenation. Then, it is sniffed.

The Prince de Talleyrand, famous diplomat of Napoleon's time, once offered a glass of precious wine to a visitor. The guest was a "nouveau-riche." He accepted the glass and drank it "bottoms up." Prince de Talleyrand was appalled. "Is this the way you drink rare wines?" he asked. "Monseigneur," answered his guest, "I must confess that I don't know how such wines should be drunk."

"Well, have another glass and do as I say: first look at the beautiful color, the limpidity of the wine, the 'fires' in it; then swirl it; then sniff it and enjoy the wonderful bouquet; then put your glass back on the table . . . and talk about it."

Two lessons may be learned from this anecdote. First, it is courteous and proper to comment on the wine your host has selected. It is like complimenting a woman on a new dress: it is a compliment to his taste which has nothing to do with the price itself.

The second lesson is that so much enjoyment is to be derived from the sight and "perfume" of the wine that the tasting and swallowing are only added pleasures and not the whole of wine drinking.

For a connoisseur drinking wine without sniffing it is like looking at a vase of beautiful roses without smelling them. Why bring pleasure to only one sense when you can gratify others at the same time?

When to Drink Wine?

French people drink wine with all meals. A French housewife would be outraged if people were to drink water with the meal she has cooked.

A fine meal without wine is like a beautiful diamond presented wrapped in a piece of brown paper. A French cook feels that it is worth her best efforts to make a delicious dish when this dish will be enhanced by a good wine. For her, it would be discouraging to work with taste and imagination in order to make a wonderful meal which will be eaten in haste and lose most of its flavor by being washed down with glasses of ice water.

Chapter II

Hors-d'Oeuvre

THE FRENCH love both to begin and end the meal with a lavish array of food. At the beginning, it is "hors-d'oeuvre variés," and at the end, a tray of different cheeses.

"Hors-d'oeuvre variés" are so appetizing that the diner may easily be carried away and eat so much of them that no more appetite is left for the main dish. Some of the restaurants which offer the largest choice of hors-d'oeuvre show two prices on their menus: one for "hors-d'oeuvre" and another for "hors-d'oeuvre only."

Many of the dishes which compose "hors-d'oeuvre variés" make excellent main dishes for luncheon or light summer dinner. And, of course, you may simply forget about their being hors-d'oeuvre and serve them as buffet dishes with one important "pièce de résistance," such as ham or turkey.

A great number of hors-d'oeuvre may be served as spreads or canapés with cocktail.

One or two hors-d'oeuvre open a family dinner deliciously and happily complete a meal otherwise too light.

Many hors-d'oeuvre require no or very little preparation. Others are more elaborate. For real "hors-d'oeuvre variés," combine a little of each.

With hors-d'oeuvre, serve:

A light dry white wine (chilled): a Bordeaux Graves; a Pouilly-Fuissé; an Alsatian Riesling or Traminer; a domestic Riesling.

Or a chilled rosé wine.

Hors-d'Oeuvre

OLIVES

Green olives, plain; or stuffed with pimiento, anchovies, or almonds. Black olives sprinkled with a few drops of olive oil.

MARINATED HERRING

Not worth making at home: some of the commercial brands are quite good.

SARDINES

Canned sardines served in their oil, decorated with wedges of lemon.

TUNA FISH

Canned in oil: serve garnished with slices of pickled cucumber or thin rings of Bermuda onions. Canned in brine: garnish with thin slices of sweet onion.

MELON

Serve with wedges of lime. Excellent with paper-thin slices of smoked ham.

RADISHES

Wash and trim. Serve with salt and butter.

CAVIAR

Black caviar: serve on ice with toast, butter, wedges of lemon. Red caviar: serve with toast, butter, wedges of lemon, sour cream, finely chopped chives, finely chopped scallions.

SMOKED SALMON

Decorate with parsley. Serve with wedges of lemon. Or sprinkle with olive oil and freshly ground pepper.

PATES

All pâtés are good for hors-d'oeuvre. Also very good as hors-d'oeuvre: salami, headcheese, ham.

SHRIMPS

Cook and shell. Cover with mayonnaise combined with lemon juice and paprika.

STUFFED EGGS

Split hard-cooked eggs lengthwise. Combine yolks with mayonnaise. Season to taste. Stuff whites with yolk mixture. Garnish with pieces of anchovy.

SALADS*

Spaghetti, dried beans, cucumber, leek, lentil, string beans, tomato, potato, rice and egg, beet, salad Madras.

EGGPLANT CAVIAR

1 eggplant	2 tablesp. lemon juice
½ teasp. salt	2 tablesp. finely chopped scallion
¼ teasp. pepper	2 tablesp. parsley
2 tablesp. olive oil	1 clove garlic, finely chopped

Bake eggplant whole and unpeeled for 1 hour at 450° F. Peel. Place eggplant in a bowl. Chop or mash. Add all of the ingredients. Mix well. Chill.

EGGS ON CANAPE

4 poached eggs	4 anchovy filets
4 slices white bread	4 tablesp. butter
pinch of cayenne pepper	

Keep eggs warm.

Cut anchovies into very small pieces. Add butter and cayenne pepper. With a fork, mix together until well blended.

* Recipes given in Chapter IX.

Toast bread. While still warm, spread with anchovy mixture. Place one egg on each slice of toast. Serve hot.
Serves 4.

ROQUEFORT CANAPES

2 tablesp. Roquefort cheese
2 tablesp. butter
pinch of cayenne pepper

2 slices white bread
2 slices bacon, cut into two
   pieces and broiled

In mixing bowl, combine cheese, butter, and cayenne pepper. Blend well together.
Toast bread. Spread toast with cheese mixture. Cut each slice in two pieces. Broil under broiler flame for 3 minutes. Cover each canapé with one piece of bacon. Serve hot.
Makes 4 canapés.

BEETS WITH CREAM

1 cup cooked (or canned)
   beets, diced
½ teasp. salt
¼ teasp. pepper

1 tablesp. lemon juice
1 teasp. prepared mustard
4 tablesp. sour cream

In mixing bowl, combine salt, pepper, lemon juice, mustard and sour cream. Blend well together. Add beets. Mix well.

PARISIAN MUSHROOMS

½ lb. small mushrooms
juice of ½ lemon
½ teasp. salt
¼ teasp. freshly ground
   pepper

1 tablesp. olive oil
1 teasp. prepared mustard
1 tablesp. chopped parsley

Wash and trim mushrooms. In small saucepan, combine mushrooms, lemon juice, salt, pepper, and oil. Cover. Cook over brisk flame for 10 minutes. Let cool in cooking juice. When cold, remove mushrooms to serving dish. To cooking juice, add mustard. Blend well. Pour over mushrooms. Sprinkle with parsley.

CELERY "BONNE FEMME"

1 medium-size apple, thinly sliced	½ teasp. salt
	¼ teasp. pepper
¾ cup celery, thinly sliced	few drops of lemon juice
1 tablesp. prepared mustard	¼ cup sour cream

In salad bowl, combine apple and celery.

In mixing bowl, combine mustard, salt, pepper, and lemon juice. Mix well. Stir in sour cream. Blend well. Add to apple-celery mixture. Toss gently but thoroughly.

FONDUE AU FROMAGE
(Cheese Fondue)

"Fondue au fromage" is popular in all eastern France, especially in the Juras and French Alps regions. It is also very popular in Switzerland and Northern Italy.

It is "la fondue" in France, "cheese fondue" in Switzerland, and "bagno caldo" ("hot bath") in Piedmont. In the Franche-Comté region of France, there is a special kind of fondue, "la cancoillote," that has much sharper taste and a pungency which is not to everybody's taste.

Cheese fondue is served as an hors-d'oeuvre. In the French Alps, it is served any time, day or night. It is the preferred between-hours meal of skiers and mountaineers.

FONDUE AU FROMAGE
(Cheese Fondue)

1½ lbs. Swiss cheese, cut into small, thin pieces	¼ teasp. freshly ground pepper
1 clove garlic	1 teasp. flour
⅓ cup dry Alsatian wine	2 tablesp. kirsch
4 anchovy filets, cut into small pieces	pinch of baking soda
	stalks of celery, trimmed

Rub inside of small heatproof casserole with garlic. Place casserole over flame, or in bottom of chafing dish. Add cheese and wine. Bring to boil, stirring constantly, until cheese is melted. Add anchovies and pepper. Dissolve flour in water. Add brandy to flour mixture. Add brandy mixture to pan and bring again to boil. Add baking soda. Mix well. Serve in casserole. Eat by helping yourself from the pan, dipping celery stalks or small pieces of French bread in the fondue.

QUICHE LORRAINE

1 9-inch pie crust, unbaked*	4 eggs, slightly beaten
1 teasp. butter	1 cup milk
3 slices Canadian bacon, ¼ inch thick, diced	1 cup heavy cream
1 medium-size onion, finely chopped	pinch of grated nutmeg
	½ teasp. salt
½ cup grated Swiss cheese	¼ teasp. pepper

Line a 9-inch pie plate with pie crust.

In a small, heavy saucepan, heat butter. Add bacon and cook for 5 minutes, or until bacon is golden brown. Remove bacon and set aside. Add onions to pan and cook for 5 minutes. Remove onions and set aside.

Cover bottom of pie crust with bacon, onions, and ¼ cup grated cheese.

In mixing bowl, combine remaining cheese, eggs, milk, cream, nutmeg, salt, and pepper. Mix well. Pour over bacon mixture. Bake at 450° F. for 15 minutes. Reduce heat to 350° and continue baking for 15 minutes longer, or until custard is well set. Serve hot.

QUICHE ROQUEFORT

1 9-inch pie crust, unbaked	1 cup cream
¼ cup crumbled roquefort cheese	¼ cup sour cream
	½ teasp. salt
5 eggs, lightly beaten	¼ teasp. pepper
1 cup milk	¼ teasp. grated nutmeg

Line a 9-inch pie plate with pie crust and bake for 5 minutes at 450° F. Sprinkle the bottom of shell with crumbled cheese. Combine the eggs, milk, cream, sour cream, salt, pepper, and nutmeg and strain over cheese.

* Recipe given on page 160. Or a dough can be made with a package of pie-crust mix, prepared as directed.

Bake for 15 minutes at 450° F. Reduce heat to 350° F. and continue baking for 10 minutes or until custard is set. Serve hot.

Use for hors-d'oeuvre, or with cocktail.

CROQUE-MONSIEUR

8 slices white bread, trimmed	4 thin slices Swiss cheese
¼ cup butter	2 eggs
4 thin slices cooked ham	1 tablesp. water

Butter slices of bread. Make four sandwiches by placing a slice of ham and a slice of Swiss cheese between two slices of bread. Tie with a string.

In a dish, combine eggs and water and beat lightly together. Dip sandwiches in egg mixture.

In large skillet, heat remaining butter. Add sandwiches and cook over medium flame for 10 minutes on each side, or until bread is golden brown and cheese is melted. Dry on paper towel. Discard string. Serve hot.

Serves 4.

Croque-Monsieur is usually served as an hors-d'oeuvre; but served with a tomato sauce and accompanied by a tossed green salad, it makes a good luncheon main dish.

WINE: *A full-bodied red wine:*
French red Bordeaux; French red Burgundy; red Côtes du Rhône; domestic claret or Burgundy; Pinot Noir; Cabernet.

PATE MAISON

¾ lb. finely ground calf liver	1 clove, crushed
½ lb. finely ground lean pork	pinch of grated nutmeg
1 teasp. salt	pinch of cayenne pepper
½ teasp. thyme	¼ cup dry white wine
1 bay leaf, crushed	1 lb. lean pork, cut into
¼ teasp. marjoram	slices ½ inch thick
½ lb. sliced bacon	

In mixing bowl, combine calf liver, ground pork, salt, thyme, bay leaf, marjoram, clove, nutmeg, cayenne pepper, and wine.

Mix well.

Line a loaf pan 9 inches long with strips of bacon. Put in a layer of ground mixture, a layer of sliced pork, another layer of ground mixture and another of pork. Cover with strips of bacon. Cover with aluminum foil. Place dish in pan of water and bake at 350° F. for 2 hours. Remove from oven and let cool before unmolding.

For serving, cut into slices approximately ½ inch thick.

Keeps well in refrigerator for at least two weeks.

WINE:　*A full-bodied red wine:*
　　　　French red Bordeaux; French red Burgundy; red Côtes du Rhône; domestic claret or Burgundy.

COUNTRY-STYLE PATE

1½ lbs. sausage meat	2 thin slices cooked ham
1 teasp. salt	1 lb. pork loin, cut into
½ teasp. freshly ground pepper	slices ½ inch thick

In mixing bowl, combine sausage meat, salt, and pepper.

In a 9-inch loaf pan, place a layer of half the sausage meat. Top with one slice of ham. Arrange slices of pork in a layer. Cover with remaining slice of ham. Fill pan with remaining sausage meat. Cover with aluminum foil. Place in pan containing water and bake at 400° F. for 2 hours. Cool before unmolding.

For serving, cut into slices approximately ½ inch thick.

Keeps well in refrigerator for two weeks.

WINE: *A full-bodied red wine:*
　　　　French red Bordeaux; French red Burgundy, red Côtes du Rhône; domestic claret or Burgundy; Pinot Noir; Cabernet.

PORK LIVER PATE

1½ lbs. finely ground pork
    liver
1½ lbs. finely ground lean
    pork
¾ lb. ground salt pork
2 eggs
1 teasp. salt

½ teasp. freshly ground
    pepper
pinch of thyme
1 bay leaf, crushed
2 tablesp. finely chopped
    onion
½ lb. sliced bacon

In mixing bowl, combine pork liver, lean pork, and
salt pork. Mix well. Add eggs. Work together until eggs
are well blended. Add salt, pepper, thyme, bay leaf, and
onion. Work well until thoroughly mixed. Line a 9-inch
loaf pan with strips of bacon. Fill with pork mixture.
Cover with strips of bacon. Place dish in pan of water and
bake at 350° F. for 2 hours. Let cool before unmolding.

For serving, cut into slices approximately ½ inch thick.
Keeps well in refrigerator for two weeks.

WINE: *A full-bodied red wine:*
        French red Bordeaux; French red Burgundy;
        red Côtes du Rhône; domestic claret or Bur-
        gundy; Pinot Noir; Cabernet.

SAUSAGE TIMBALE
(Sausage Pâté in Crust)

1 package pie-crust mix
1½ lbs. pork sausage
2 medium-size onions,
    chopped

1 tablesp. flour
1½ cups consommé
2 eggs, beaten

8 slices white bread, crumbled

Prepare mix as directed. Roll out two-thirds of dough
to fit a loaf pan (8″x5″x3″). Line the pan with rolled
dough. In large, heavy skillet, cook sausages until slightly
browned. Remove sausages and set aside. Pour fat off
skillet, leaving only 1 tablespoon of fat. Add onions to
skillet and cook until slightly browned. Sprinkle with
flour and cook, stirring constantly until well browned.
Stir in consommé, and cook until smooth. Off fire, stir
in eggs.

In lined loaf pan, place a layer of sausages. Cover with

layer of approximately 1 inch of bread crumbs. Pour 3
to 4 tablespoons of sauce from skillet over crumbs. Fill
pan, alternating layers of sausages and bread crumbs
moistened with sauce, finishing with bread-crumb layer.

Roll out remaining dough into a rectangle about ½
inch larger than top of pan. Place over bread-crumb
layer, pressing edges together. Bake at 350° F. for 1½
hours. Unmold.

WINE: *A light red wine:*
        Red Bordeaux; Beaujolais; domestic claret.
        Or a chilled dry white wine:
        Pouilly-Fuissé; white Côtes du Rhône;
        Alsatian Riesling; Pinot Blanc.
        Or a rosé wine.

Chapter III

Soup

ONION SOUP

IF THERE is one French dish which is popular all over the world, in all categories of restaurants, it is onion soup. Every day, everywhere, people expectantly order onion soup, but what they too often get is a sorry brew, the result of a long series of deteriorations of the original recipe.

Honest-to-goodness onion soup is neither expensive nor difficult to make. The important thing is that the taste of onion is well blended and not bitter or harsh. The soup has the consistency of light cream and is of a golden color. It is not a clear broth in which float small pieces of dark and desiccated onion and a few specks of grated cheese. Grated cheese may be added at the table, but a sufficient quantity has to cook in the soup itself.

Note that the slices of bread should be dried in a heated oven after the flame has been turned off. Do not toast them.

With proper care, you will get a smooth, soothing, golden soup, which succeeds in being both pungent and delicate—no small achievement indeed!

3 medium-size onions,
    thinly sliced
2 tablesp. butter
1 tablesp. flour
2 cups consommé
4 cups water

¼ cup boiled milk
¼ lb. grated Swiss cheese
6 dried slices French bread
salt and pepper to taste
2 tablesp. melted butter

In heavy skillet, cook onions in heated butter until slightly browned. Sprinkle with flour and cook over low flame until golden, never allowing them to become dark brown. Add consommé and water. Bring to boil, stirring constantly with a wooden spoon, then simmer gently for 20 minutes uncovered. Add milk. Pour into ovenproof casserole or individual bowls. Place slices of bread on top. Sprinkle generously with cheese. Add pepper. Sprinkle with melted butter. Brown quickly under broiler flame. Serves 4 to 6.

WINE: *A light red wine:*
        Red Bordeaux; Beaujolais; domestic claret.
        Or a chilled dry white wine:
        Pouilly-Fuissé; white Côtes du Rhône;
        Alsatian Riesling; Pinot Blanc.
        Or a rosé wine.

POT-AU-FEU

Pot-au-feu is more than a soup. It is a French national institution. In many families there is a "Pot-au-Feu Day" each week. The funny part about it is that everybody accepts it but nobody entirely approves of it, though it may be for opposite reasons.

In every family there are the ones who like the bouillon but resent being served the meat and vegetables as the main dish, and others who like the meat and vegetables but don't care for the bouillon twice a week. (One pot-au-feu makes enough bouillon for two meals.) Hence the creation of "petite marmite" which seems to please everybody except the housewife, because petite marmite is more expensive, being served only as a soup and requires more service since it is served individually.

In this country we can forget about the sentimental connotation of pot-au-feu and treat it as any other good dish without feeling an obligation to serve it regularly. When eaten less often it is a truly magnificent meal. The bouillon is excellent. The meat and vegetables are delicious when cooked to the exact degree of perfection and served with an appetizing variety of mustard, pickles, relishes, etc. With a salad, a chunk of cheese, and a glass of wine, this makes a well-balanced satisfying, and nourishing meal.

4 carrots	2 tablesp. salt
1 white turnip	4½ quarts water
¼ of yellow turnip	1 large onion, stuck with
6 leeks (white part only)	2 cloves
1 stalk celery	1 small bay leaf
4 lbs. rump of beef	¼ teasp. thyme
1 veal knuckle	1 clove garlic (optional)
4 lbs. beef bones	

8 thin slices French bread, dried (but not toasted) in warm oven

Clean vegetables and cut them into desired size.

In a large soup kettle, place beef, knuckle, bones, and salt. Cover with water. Bring to boil, then simmer for 2 hours, skimming the scum off frequently. Add vegetables, onion, bay leaf, thyme, and garlic, and continue simmering for 1½ hours longer. Skim fat off bouillon. Serve bouillon with slices of dry French bread.

Meat and vegetables are served as main course. Meat is cut into thin slices and served surrounded by the vegetables.

Serves 6 to 8.

WINE: *A red wine:*
      Red Bordeaux; French red Burgundy; red Côtes du Rhône; domestic claret or Burgundy.

PETITE MARMITE

Petite marmite is prepared in exactly the same way as pot-au-feu. The only difference is in the serving.

The meat is cut into small pieces and is served with

the vegetables and bouillon in individual casseroles. On top of each casserole, place a slice of French bread sprinkled with grated Swiss cheese. Place under broiler flame for 2 to 3 minutes, until cheese is melted and browned.

POTATO AND LEEK SOUP

2 tablesp. butter	1 tablesp. salt
3 medium-size leeks (white part only)	1 egg yolk
	1 cup milk
1½ lbs. potatoes, peeled and quartered	6 slices French bread, fried in butter
6 cups water	

Heat butter in kettle or large saucepan. Shred leeks and add to pan. Cook until leeks are slightly browned. Add potatoes, water, and salt. Bring to boil. Cover and simmer for 30 minutes, or until potatoes are tender. Strain. Mash vegetables. Stir cooking liquid into mashed vegetables and return to pan. Bring to boil. Stir in milk and yolk. Bring back to boiling point but do not allow to boil. Serve hot with fried French bread, or chilled without bread.
Serves 4.

SORREL SOUP

½ lb. sorrel	1 tablesp. salt
2 tablesp. butter	1 cup milk
6 cups water	1 egg yolk
½ lb. potatoes, peeled and quartered	6 slices French bread, fried in butter

Clean and shred sorrel. Chop coarsely. In kettle or large saucepan, heat butter. Add sorrel and cook, stirring constantly, for 10 minutes, or until sorrel is reduced to approximately ½ cup. Add water, potatoes, and salt. Bring to boil. Cover and simmer for 30 minutes. Strain. Mash vegetables. Stir cooking liquid into mashed vegetables and return to pan. Bring to boil. Stir in milk and

yolk. Bring back to boiling point but do not allow to
boil. Serve hot with fried French bread, or chilled without bread.

Serves 4.

WATERCRESS SOUP

2 cups watercress, cleaned
  and trimmed
1 lb. potatoes, peeled
  and quartered
1 tablesp. salt
6 cups water

1 cup milk
6 slices French bread, dried
  (but not toasted) in a
  warm oven
1 tablesp. butter

In kettle or large saucepan, combine watercress, potatoes, salt, and water. Bring to boil. Cover and simmer
for 30 minutes, or until potatoes are fully cooked. Strain,
reserving liquid. Mash vegetables. Stir cooking liquid
into mashed vegetables and return to pan. Bring to boil.
Stir in milk. Bring back to boiling point but do not allow
to boil.

Butter slices of bread and place them in bottom of
soup tureen.

Pour soup over bread. Serve hot. Also good served
chilled, but without bread.

Serves 4.

GARBURE
(Country-Style Soup)

3 tablesp. butter
2 medium-size carrots, sliced
3 leeks (white part only) cut
  into pieces 1 inch long
2 cups chopped cabbage
2 stalks celery, cut into
  pieces 1 inch long
1 teasp. salt
½ teasp. granulated sugar

4 cups water
3 cups consommé
1 cup cooked dried navy or
  white beans
2 medium-size potatoes,
  sliced
3 tablesp. green peas
6 slices French bread fried in
  butter

grated Swiss cheese

In large, heavy saucepan, combine butter, carrots, leeks,
cabbage, celery, salt, and sugar. Cover and cook over a low

flame for 30 minutes. Add water and consommé. Bring
to boil. Add beans, potatoes, and peas. Cover. Simmer for
45 minutes. Remove vegetables and mash them. Place
mashed vegetable mixture in tureen. Stir liquid in pan
into mixture. Correct seasoning to taste. Serve with slices
of fried bread and grated Swiss cheese.

Serves 4 to 6.

SHRIMP BISQUE

½ lb. shrimps, shelled and de-veined	1 teasp. salt
	¼ teasp. pepper
1 tablesp. butter	pinch of thyme
¼ cup brandy	1 hard-cooked egg
2 cups water	2 tablesp. tomato paste
1 cup dry white wine	½ teasp. paprika

Heat butter in large, heavy saucepan. Add shrimps
and cook over brisk flame for 5 minutes. Add brandy.
Ignite. Add water, wine, salt, pepper, and thyme. Bring
to boil. Cover and simmer for 15 minutes. Remove
shrimps and set aside.

Mash together shrimps, hard-cooked egg, and ½ cup
of cooking liquid. Add tomato paste and paprika. Stir
in remaining cooking liquid and return to pan. Correct
seasoning.

Heat. Serve hot.

Serves 4.

SOUP CRECY

1 lb. carrots, sliced	1 lump sugar
3 tablesp. butter	1 tablesp. finely chopped parsley
4 large potatoes, peeled and quartered	4 slices French bread, diced and fried in butter
1 tablesp. salt	
6 cups water	

In kettle or large saucepan, combine carrots and 2
tablespoons of butter. Cover and cook over low flame
for 20 minutes. Add potatoes, salt, water, and sugar.

Bring to boil. Cover and simmer for 45 minutes. Strain, reserving liquid. Mash vegetables. Stir cooking liquid into mashed vegetables and return to pan. Bring to boil and simmer for 15 minutes. Off fire, add remaining butter cut into small pieces, stirring until butter is melted and well blended. Sprinkle with parsley. Serve hot with fried diced bread.

Serves 4.

PUMPKIN SOUP

2 cups pumpkin, trimmed and diced
2 cups water
1 teasp. salt
4 cups milk

1½ tablesp. granulated sugar
6 slices French bread, dried in warm oven (but not toasted)

2 tablesp. butter, cut into small pieces

In kettle or large saucepan, combine pumpkin, water, and salt. Bring to boil. Cover and simmer for 15 minutes. Strain, reserving liquid. Mash pumpkin. Stir in cooking liquid. Return to pan. Add milk, sugar, and bread cut into small pieces. Bring to boil. Cover and simmer for 10 minutes. Off fire, add butter, stirring until butter is melted and well blended. Serve hot.

Serves 4.

TOMATO SOUP

1 tablesp. butter
1 large onion, chopped
6 tomatoes, peeled and quartered
1 large potato, peeled and quartered

6 cups water
1 bay leaf
small piece of garlic
1 teasp. salt
¼ cup rice

Heat butter in kettle or large saucepan. Add onion and cook for 10 minutes, or until onion is browned. Add tomatoes and continue cooking for 10 minutes, stirring frequently. Add potatoes, 2 cups water, bay leaf, garlic, and salt. Bring to boil. Cover and simmer for 20 minutes.

Add remaining water. Bring again to boil. Discard garlic and bay leaf. Strain, reserving liquid. Mash vegetables. Stir in cooking liquid. Return to pan. Bring to boil. Add rice. Cover and simmer for 15 minutes. Serve hot, in soup plates or individual cups.

Serves 4.

BEAN SOUP

¾ lb. white dried beans,
   soaked overnight
6 cups lukewarm water
1 teasp. salt
1 large onion, studded with
   1 clove
1 carrot
1 bay leaf
pinch of thyme
1 2-inch piece of celery
1 cup scalded milk
2 tablesp. butter, cut into
   small pieces
4 slices French bread, diced
   and fried in butter

In kettle or large saucepan, combine beans, water, salt, onion, carrot, bay leaf, thyme, and celery. Bring to boil. Cover and simmer for 2 hours, or until beans are very tender. Discard carrot, bay leaf, and celery. Drain, reserving liquid. Mash beans. Stir in cooking liquid. Return to pan. Add milk. Bring to boiling point but do not allow to boil. Off fire, add butter, stirring until butter is melted and well blended. Serve hot, with fried diced bread.

Serves 4.

POTAGE CHAMONIX

1 cup leftover chicken
2 tablesp. blanched almonds
3 yolks of hard-cooked eggs
2 cups clear chicken broth
2 cups water
¼ cup heavy cream
½ teasp. salt
¼ teasp. white pepper
4 slices French bread, fried
   in butter

Grind chicken and almonds. Stir in chopped yolks. Mix well. Gradually stir in chicken broth, water, cream, salt, and pepper. Heat in top of double boiler. Serve with fried bread.

Serves 4.

CAULIFLOWER CREAM SOUP

¾ lb. cauliflower, cleaned and trimmed

4 large potatoes, peeled and cut into small pieces

6 cups scalded milk

1 teasp. salt

2 tablesp. butter, cut into small pieces

4 slices French bread, diced and fried in butter

1 teasp. finely chopped parsley

In boiling salted water, cook cauliflower for 5 minutes. Drain. In kettle or large saucepan, combine cauliflower, potatoes, 4 cups milk, and salt. Bring to boil. Cover and simmer for 30 minutes. Strain, reserving liquid. Mash vegetables. Stir in cooking liquid. Return to pan. Add remaining milk. Bring to boil. Off fire, add butter, stirring until butter is melted and well blended. Place fried diced bread in bottom of soup tureen. Pour soup over it. Serve hot.

Serves 4.

Chapter IV

Eggs and Omelets

FRENCH OMELETS are famous for their smoothness and lightness. This is because the eggs are cooked very quickly and remain moist—as they should. Once the butter is hot, it does not take more than two minutes to make the omelet itself.

There is in every French household an "omelet skillet," used only for that purpose. It is a cast-iron or heavy aluminum skillet, approximately 9 inches across. It is never washed but is carefully wiped after each use with paper towels. If it becomes necessary to wash it, it is scoured with a scouring pad, then oiled and wiped with paper.

Some omelet skillets are larger for bigger omelets, but it is never advisable to make an omelet of more than 4 eggs. It is much easier to cook two 3-egg omelets than a 6-egg one.

The eggs should be taken out of the refrigerator one hour before cooking. They are beaten lightly, just enough to break them and blend the whites and yolks together. This is done at the last minute.

The one essential factor in the successful making of an omelet is the temperature of the butter. The eggs are not poured into the skillet until the butter bubbles and turns "noisette" (hazelnut), that is, slightly brown. Then the eggs are turned into the skillet and the omelet is briskly made.

Many cooks, just before serving, rub a piece of butter over the top of the omelet to give it a "shine," which does not make it any better but does make it more appetizing.

BASIC OMELET

4 eggs	½ teasp. salt
1 tablesp. cream	1 tablesp. butter

Combine eggs, milk, and salt in bowl. Beat gently. Place butter in skillet and heat until butter is very slightly browned. Add eggs and immediately stir them briskly with back of fork. When the eggs have thickened and there are no more liquid eggs in skillet, stop stirring and continue cooking for a few seconds, gently shaking the pan back and forth over the heat. Take skillet off fire and with a fork fold one-third of omelet over center. Then fold other third over first. Slide omelet onto heated serving dish.

Serves 2.

WINE: *A chilled dry white wine:*
         Bordeaux Graves; Alsatian Riesling;
         Pouilly-Fuissé; French chablis; Pinot Blanc.

OMELET WITH CHICKEN LIVERS

egg mixture (as in "basic omelet")	½ cup chicken livers, sliced
1 tablesp. butter	2 tablesp. clear chicken broth
	1 tablesp. manié butter*

In small skillet, heat butter. Add chicken livers and cook over brisk flame for 5 minutes, or until livers are browned. Add chicken broth. Bring to boil. Add manié

* Recipe given on page 125.

butter and continue cooking for 2 minutes, or until sauce thickens.

Meanwhile, make omelet as in "basic omelet." Before folding it, place liver mixture in center. Fold omelet over livers.

WINE: *A light red wine:*
  Red Bordeaux; Beaujolais; domestic claret.
  Or a chilled dry white wine:
  Pouilly-Fuissé; white Côtes du Rhône;
  Alsatian Riesling; Pinot Blanc.
  Or a rosé wine.

ONION OMELET

egg mixture (as in "basic omelet")   2 tablesp. butter
    2 tablesp. chopped onions

In omelet skillet, heat 1 tablespoon butter. Add onions and cook for 5 minutes, or until onions are slightly browned. Add remaining butter. Heat until butter is slightly browned.

Add egg mixture and make omelet as in "basic omelet."

WINE: *A light red wine:*
  Red Bordeaux; Beaujolais; domestic claret.
  Or a chilled dry white wine:
  Pouilly-Fuissé; white Côtes du Rhône;
  Alsatian Riesling; Pinot Blanc.
  Or a rosé wine.

OMELET WITH HERBS

egg mixture (as in "basic omelet")   1 tablesp. chives, finely chopped
    1 tablesp. parsley, finely chopped

To egg mixture, add chives and parsley. Mix well. Make omelet according to recipe of "basic omelet."

WINE: *A chilled dry white wine:*
  Bordeaux Graves; Alsatian Riesling;
  Pouilly-Fuissé; French chablis; Pinot Blanc.

OMELET WITH CROUTONS

egg mixture (as in "basic   ½ cup French bread cut into
   omelet")   ½-inch cubes
2 tablesp. butter

Heat butter in small skillet. Add bread and cook over
medium flame until bread is well browned on all sides.
To egg mixture, add fried bread. Mix well.
Make omelet according to recipe of "basic omelet."
WINE: *A light red wine:*
      Red Bordeaux; Beaujolais; domestic claret.
      Or a chilled dry white wine:
      Pouilly-Fuissé; white Côtes du Rhône;
      Alsatian Riesling; Pinot Blanc.
      Or a rosé wine.

TUNA FISH OMELET

In this recipe the omelet is usually made with oil instead of butter.

egg mixture (as in "basic   ⅛ cup canned tuna fish,
   omelet")   cut into small pieces
          1 tablesp. vegetable oil

Add tuna fish to egg mixture. In omelet skillet, heat
oil until it is hot. Make omelet as in "basic omelet."
WINE: *A chilled dry white wine:*
      Bordeaux Graves; Alsatian Riesling;
      Pouilly-Fuissé; French chablis; Pinot Blanc.

HAM OMELET

egg mixture (as in "basic   1 tablesp. butter
   omelet")   ⅛ cup diced cooked ham

In small, heavy skillet, heat butter. Add ham and cook
for 10 minutes, or until ham is well browned. Add ham
to egg mixture and make omelet as in "basic omelet."
WINE: *A chilled dry white wine:*
      Bordeaux Graves; Alsatian Riesling;
      Pouilly-Fuissé; French chablis; Pinot Blanc.

OMELET COUNTRY STYLE

egg mixture (as in "basic   1 tablesp. butter
   omelet")   ⅛ lb. salt pork, diced
                         2 boiled potatoes, diced

In omelet skillet, heat butter. Add salt pork and potatoes and cook for 15 minutes, or until golden brown. Add
omelet mixture to pan and make omelet. Fold omelet in
two or serve flat.

WINE: *A chilled dry white wine:*
         Bordeaux Graves; Alsatian Riesling;
         Pouilly-Fuissé; French chablis; Pinot Blanc.

SORREL OMELET

egg mixture (as in "basic   1 tablesp. butter
   omelet")   ¼ teasp. salt
1 cup sorrel, cleaned and
   trimmed

Shred sorrel. In small, heavy saucepan, heat butter.
Add sorrel and salt, and cook for 10 minutes, stirring
constantly.

Add to egg mixture and make omelet as in "basic
omelet."

OMELET PARMENTIER

egg mixture (as in "basic   3 medium-size boiled
   omelet")   potatoes
                         2 tablesp. butter

Dice potatoes. In heavy skillet, heat butter. Add potatoes and cook for 15 minutes, or until potatoes are golden
brown. Add potatoes to egg mixture and make omelet
as in "basic omelet."

WINE: *A chilled dry white wine:*
         Bordeaux Graves; Alsatian Riesling;
         Pouilly-Fuissé; French chablis; Pinot Blanc.

PIPERADE

"Piperade" is a very special kind of omelet which is made in a variety of ways, in the whole South of France. Its popularity is spreading a little more every year and has recently reached as far north as Paris.

4 slices bacon, cut into small pieces
1 large onion, sliced
4 slices Canadian bacon, cut into small pieces
4 green peppers, cut into strips ½ inch wide
1 1-lb–12-oz. can tomatoes, drained and mashed
1 clove garlic, crushed

½ teasp. salt
¼ teasp. freshly ground pepper
2 tablesp. fresh bread crumbs
1 tablesp. butter
8 eggs, slightly beaten
4 slices French bread, fried in butter

Heat bacon in large, heavy skillet. Add onions and cook until they become transparent. Add Canadian bacon, peppers, tomatoes, garlic, salt, and pepper. Cook for 30 minutes, stirring occasionally. Add bread crumbs and continue cooking for 15 minutes.

In another heavy skillet, heat butter. Add eggs and cook briskly, stirring gently with a fork, until eggs are set. Stir in mixture from other skillet. Garnish with fried bread. Serve hot.

Serves 4.

WINE: *A chilled dry white wine:*
Bordeaux Graves; Alsatian Riesling;
Pouilly-Fuissé; French chablis; Pinot Blanc.

EGGS BERCY

4 eggs
½ teasp. salt
¼ teasp. freshly ground pepper

2 tablesp. tomato sauce
4 small pork sausages, cooked

Butter a pie dish. Break eggs in dish. Add salt and pepper. Bake at 400° F. for 15 minutes. Arrange tomato sauce and sausages between yolks. Continue baking for 5 minutes. Serve hot in baking dish.

Serves 4.

WINE: *A chilled dry white wine:*
Bordeaux Graves; Alsatian Riesling;
Pouilly-Fuissé; French chablis; Pinot Blanc.

EGGS A LA TRIPE

8 hard-cooked eggs	1 cup scalded milk
3 tablesp. butter	1 teasp. salt
2 small onions, finely chopped	¼ teasp. white pepper pinch of grated nutmeg
2 tablesp. flour	2 sprigs parsley

Melt 2 tablespoons butter in small, heavy saucepan. Add onions. Cover and cook over low flame for 20 minutes. Add flour, and cook for 5 minutes, stirring constantly. Do not allow flour to brown. Stir in milk. Add salt, pepper, grated nutmeg, and parsley. Cook over low flame for 15 minutes. Discard parsley.

Split eggs lengthwise and add to pan. Continue cooking for 5 minutes. Off fire, add remaining butter, cut into small pieces. Serve hot in heated round dish.

Serves 4.

WINE: *A chilled dry white wine:*
Bordeaux Graves; Alsatian Riesling;
Pouilly-Fuissé; French chablis; Pinot Blanc.

EGGS LORRAINE

4 eggs	¼ cup sour cream
4 slices Canadian bacon	½ teasp. salt
2 thin slices Swiss cheese cut into 2 pieces	¼ teasp. white pepper

Lay bacon in a pie dish. Place slices of Swiss cheese over bacon. Break eggs on top of cheese. Add salt and pepper. Cover with sour cream. Bake at 400° F. for 20 minutes, or until whites are well set. Serve hot in dish.

Serves 4.

WINE: *A chilled dry white wine:*
         Bordeaux Graves; Alsatian Riesling;
         Pouilly-Fuissé; French chablis; Pinot Blanc.

EGGS COCOTTE

3 tablesp. butter	1 teasp. flour
½ cup mushrooms, coarsely chopped	¼ cup chicken broth
	4 eggs
pinch of cayenne pepper	½ teasp. salt

In small skillet, heat 1 tablespoon butter. Add mushrooms and cook for 2 minutes over high flame, stirring constantly. Add ¼ teaspoon salt and cayenne pepper. Sprinkle with flour and cook until slightly browned. Add chicken broth. Lower flame and simmer for 5 minutes.

Butter 4 custard cups with remaining butter. Place 1 tablespoon mushrooms at bottom of each cup. Break 1 egg in each cup over mushrooms. Salt. Place cups in pan containing hot water. Bake at 400° F. for approximately 10 minutes, or until white is well set. Serve hot.

(If eggs are taken from refrigerator just before cooking, baking time is about 5 minutes longer.)

WINE: *A chilled dry white wine:*
         Bordeaux Graves; Alsatian Riesling;
         Pouilly-Fuissé; French chablis; Pinot Blanc.

CHEESE SOUFFLE

2 tablesp. butter	pinch of grated nutmeg
2 tablesp. flour	4 egg yolks
¾ cup milk	1 cup shredded Swiss cheese
½ teasp. salt	5 egg whites
¼ teasp. freshly ground pepper	

Melt butter in heavy saucepan over low flame. Stir in flour. Add milk, salt, pepper, and nutmeg, stirring constantly until smooth and thickened. Take pan off fire and stir in yolks one at a time. Add cheese. Mix well. Return pan to fire and, stirring constantly, cook over a low flame for 10 minutes, or until cheese is melted. Let cool slightly.

Beat egg whites until they are stiff, and fold them into cheese mixture. Pour batter into a buttered soufflé dish. Bake in oven at 375° F. for 30 minutes. Serve immediately.

Serves 4.

WINE: *A chilled dry white wine:*
Bordeaux Graves; Alsatian Riesling;
Pouilly-Fuissé; French chablis; Pinot Blanc.

Chapter V

Fish

THERE IS A SAYING in France, "La sauce fait passer le poisson." Which means, "The sauce is what makes fish palatable." It has even a figurative sense, and is often used to mean that the right way to do or say something makes it acceptable or pleasant.

France is a man's country and French cooking has developed around men's taste. As in most countries, Frenchmen prefer meat, and fish never seems to fill their idea of a hearty and tasty meal. As a result, except when freshly caught, fish is always elaborately prepared so as to make it a delicacy. When just out of the water, the simplest way of cooking it (grilled or broiled) is just considered the best.

There is a tremendous variety of fish in France because the country is bordered on three sides by four different bodies of water: the North Sea, The Channel, the Atlantic Ocean, and the Mediterranean Sea, each with its specific marine fauna. And there are innumerable rivers and lakes.

Faced with such a tremendous choice in fish and little

taste to eat it, the French have developed the most delectable ways of cooking it.

Although fish in the United States are of different kinds, most of them may be prepared in the same manner.

FISH COURT-BOUILLON

In general, made with fresh-water fish: trout, pike, carp, etc.

1 to 1½ lbs. fish	1 bay leaf
2 quarts water	½ teasp. thyme
¼ cup wine vinegar	5 sprigs parsley
2 medium-size carrots, sliced	1 tablesp. salt
2 large onions, sliced	8 peppercorns

In kettle or large saucepan, combine all ingredients except fish and peppercorns. Bring to boil. Cover and simmer for 40 minutes. Let cool. When ready to use, heat Court-bouillon until luke warm. Add peppercorns and fish. Bring to boiling point but do not allow to boil, and continue cooking for 10 minutes. Remove fish to heated serving dish. Serve hot.

Serves 4.

If the fish is to be served cold, let it cool in Court-bouillon and remove it just before serving.

FISH MEUNIERE

Made with small fish: sole, sole filets, codfish, whitefish, herring, mackerel, trout, etc.; or with slices of large fish: salmon, swordfish, etc.

1 to 1½ lbs. fish	¼ cup flour
1 teasp. salt	4 tablesp. butter
½ teasp. pepper	few drops of lemon juice
	1 tablesp. chopped parsley

Salt and pepper fish. Dredge fish with flour. In large, heavy skillet, heat two tablespoons butter until it begins to turn slightly brown. Add fish, leaving a little space between pieces so they do not touch. Lower flame. Cook over very low flame for 5 minutes. Turn fish and cook for 5 minutes on the other side. Remove fish to heated serving dish and keep warm. Add 2 tablespoons butter to skillet and cook until butter is slightly browned. Sprinkle fish with lemon juice and parsley. Pour butter from skillet over fish. Serve very hot.

Serves 4.

WINE: *A chilled white wine:*
DRY: Bordeaux Graves; Alsatian Riesling or Traminer; Sauvignon Blanc.
SWEET: Bordeaux Sauternes; Gewurztraminer; sweet Semillon.

FISH MAITRE D'HOTEL

1 to 1½ lbs. filets of fish	1 teasp. salt
(4 to 6 pieces)	1 lemon, cut into thin slices
2 cups water	

In large saucepan, combine water and salt. Add fillets. Bring to boil. Take pan off fire and let stand, covered, for 10 minutes. Remove fish to heated serving dish. Garnish with slices of lemon. Serve hot.

Serve with maître d'hôtel butter*, to which a pinch of dried tarragon leaves has been added.

Serves 4 to 6.

WINE: *A chilled white wine:*
DRY: Bordeaux Graves; Alsatian Riesling or Traminer; Sauvignon Blanc.
SWEET: Bordeaux Sauternes; Gewurztraminer; sweet Semillon.

FISH FILETS LE HAVRE

1 to 1½ lbs. filets of fish	3 tablesp. butter
(4 to 6 pieces)	2 tablesp. whisky
½ teasp. salt	2 tablesp. heavy cream
¼ teasp. pepper	2 tablesp. bottled clam
2 tablesp. paprika	juice
¼ cup flour	2 tablesp. lemon juice

Salt and pepper filets. Dredge with paprika and then with flour. In large, heavy skillet, heat 2 tablespoons but-

* Recipe given on page 130.

ter. Add filets and cook 5 minutes on each side. Remove
filets to heated serving dish and keep warm. Pour fat off
skillet. Add whisky to skillet and ignite. Lower flame. Add
cream and clam juice and cook for 3 minutes. Take skillet
off fire. Add lemon juice and remaining butter, cut into
small pieces, stirring constantly until well blended. Pour
sauce over filets. Serve hot.

Serves 4 to 6.

WINE: *A chilled white wine:*
DRY: Bordeaux Graves; Alsatian Riesling or Traminer;
        Sauvignon Blanc.
SWEET: Bordeaux Sauternes; Gewurztraminer; sweet
        Semillon.

FISH FILETS "GOURMET"

1 to 1½ lbs. filets of fish	1 small bay leaf
2 tablesp. finely chopped onion	1 teasp. salt
	¼ teasp. pepper
1 medium-size carrot, sliced	1 cup dry white wine
1 medium-size lemon, sliced	⅛ cup French vermouth
pinch of thyme	1 tablesp. chopped parsley

In greased baking dish, combine onions, carrot, lemon,
thyme, bay leaf, salt, and pepper. Add filets. Add wine
and vermouth. Bake at 400° F. for 20 minutes. Sprinkle
with parsley. Serve hot in baking dish.

Serves 4 to 6.

Good with all white-meated fish.

WINE: *A chilled dry white wine:*
        Bordeaux Graves; Alsatian Riesling; Pouilly-
        Fuissé; French chablis; Pinot Blanc.

FISH FILETS WITH MUSHROOMS

1 to 1½ lbs. filets of fish	¼ teasp. pepper
1 tablesp. finely chopped onion	1 cup dry white wine
	⅔ cup bottled clam juice
1 4-oz. can sliced mushrooms and juice	2 tablesp. butter
1 tablesp. chopped parsley	2 tablesp. flour
½ teasp. salt	2 teasp. lemon juice
	2 tablesp. sour cream

In greased baking dish, place onions, mushrooms and juice, parsley, folded or rolled filets, salt, and pepper. Add wine and clam juice. Cover with wax paper and bake at 400° F. for 30 minutes. Remove filets to heated serving dish and keep warm.

In small saucepan, heat butter. Stir in flour. Add liquid from baked fish and cook, stirring until smooth and thickened. Stir in lemon juice and sour cream. Cook over low flame for 5 minutes. Pour over filets. Serve hot.

Serves 4 to 6.

WINE: *A chilled white wine:*

DRY: Bordeaux Graves; Alsatian Riesling or Traminer; Sauvignon Blanc.

SWEET: Bordeaux Sauternes; Gewurztraminer; sweet Semillon.

FISH COTE-D'AZUR

1 tablesp. olive oil	1 small bay leaf
1 to 1½ lbs. fish steaks (4 to 6 pieces)	½ clove garlic, crushed
	4 peppercorns
4 tomatoes, peeled and quartered	½ teasp. salt
	¼ teasp. saffron
pinch of fennel seeds	1 cup dry white wine
pinch of thyme	1 lemon

Oil a large skillet. Place fish in skillet. Add tomatoes, fennel, thyme, bay leaf, garlic, peppercorns, salt, and saffron. Add wine. Bring to boil. Cover and simmer for 10 minutes, or until fish is well cooked but still firm. Cool fish in cooking liquid. Serve fish cold with 4 to 6 tablespoons of cooking liquid. Garnish with thin slices of lemon.

Serves 4 to 6.

Good for firm-meated fish: swordfish, tuna fish, salmon, etc.

WINE: *A chilled dry white wine:*

Bordeaux Graves; Alsatian Riesling; Pouilly-Fuissé; French chablis; Pinot Blanc.

FISH SIBERIAN*

1 to 1½ lbs. fish steaks (4 pieces)	3 tablesp. butter
1 teasp. salt	2 tablesp. scallion, chopped
¼ teasp. freshly ground pepper	4 tablesp. sour cream
	1 tablesp. lemon juice
	¼ teasp. white pepper

Season fish with black pepper and ½ teaspoon salt. Spread fish with 2 tablespoons butter. Place fish on oiled broiler and broil under broiler flame for 3 minutes on one side, and 2 minutes on the other side.

Meanwhile, in a small saucepan, heat remaining butter. Add scallion and cook until slightly browned. Lower flame. Stir in sour cream and lemon juice. Add remaining salt and white pepper. Simmer for 3 minutes. Remove fish to heated serving dish. Cover fish with cream sauce from pan. Serve hot.

Serves 4.

WINE: *A chilled white wine:*

DRY: Bordeaux Graves; Alsatian Riesling or Traminer; Sauvignon Blanc.

SWEET: Bordeaux Sauternes; Gewurztraminer; sweet Semillon.

FISH "COCOTE"

1½ to 2 lbs. swordfish or tuna (fresh or frozen)	1 teasp. salt
3 tablesp. butter	1 bay leaf
½ lb. small white onions	pinch of pepper
1 cup Alsatian Riesling wine	pinch of thyme
	1 tablesp. flour

In Dutch oven or large, heavy saucepan, heat 2 tablespoons butter. Add fish and onions, and cook until fish is well browned on all sides. Add wine, salt, pepper, bay leaf, and thyme. Bring to boil. Cover and simmer for 40 minutes. Remove fish to heated serving dish and keep warm. Work together remaining butter and flour, and

* There's nothing Russian about "Fish Siberian." It is called so because the sauce covers it with a white "blanket" and, for the French, Siberia is the whitest of all the white wildernesses. If you ask them, summer, winter, spring, or fall, Siberia is white and covered with a heavy blanket of snow.

add mixture to pan. Cook for a few seconds until sauce thickens. Pour over fish. Serve hot, with boiled potatoes. Serves 4 to 6.

WINE: *A chilled dry white wine:*
Bordeaux Graves; Alsatian Riesling; Pouilly-Fuissé; French chablis; Pinot Blanc.

FISH "BASQUE"

4 tablesp. butter	2 tablesp. chopped parsley
1 to 1½ lbs. fish filets (or steaks)	½ teasp. salt
¼ cup bottled clam juice	3 tablesp. chopped scallions (white part only)
½ cup dry white wine	2 sprigs parsley
½ cup drained and mashed canned tomatoes	pinch of thyme
	1 bay leaf

¼ teasp. freshly ground pepper

Grease large skillet with 1 tablespoon butter. Lay fish in skillet. Add clam juice, wine, tomatoes, chopped parsley, scallions, salt, sprigs of parsley, thyme, and bay leaf. Cover. Cook over medium flame for 15 minutes. Discard parsley and bay leaf. Remove fish to heated serving dish and keep warm. Raise heat under skillet and cook, without allowing to boil, until liquid is reduced to approximately 3 tablespoons. Off fire, add pepper and remaining butter cut into small pieces. Stir until well blended. Pour sauce over fish. Serve hot.

Serves 4 to 6.

Good for filets or thin steaks of white-meated fish. Also good with swordfish and salmon.

WINE: *A chilled dry white wine:*
Muscadet; Bordeaux Graves; French chablis; Pouilly-Fuissé; white Côtes du Rhône.

FISH MINUTE

1 to 1½ lbs. filets of fish	2 tablesp. parsley
1 teasp. salt	1 cup dry white wine
¼ teasp. pepper	2 tablesp. fresh bread crumbs
2 tablesp. chopped scallions (white part only)	

Arrange filets in baking dish. Season with salt and pepper. Sprinkle with scallions and parsley. Add wine. Sprinkle with bread crumbs. Dot with butter. Bake at 450° F. for 15 minutes, or until top is browned. Serve hot in cooking dish.

Serves 4 to 6.

Good for all white-meated fish.

WINE: *A chilled dry white wine:*
Bordeaux Graves; Alsatian Riesling; Pouilly-Fuissé; French chablis; Pinot Blanc.

SHAD LOIRE

3 lbs. shad (before boning)	⅓ cup salad oil
3 cups cooked sorrel	2 tablesp. butter
½ teasp. salt	2 tablesp. lemon juice
¼ teasp. freshly ground pepper	4 hard-cooked eggs
	4 thin slices lemon

Bone shad. Season with salt and pepper. Brush with oil. Broil under flame of broiler for 3 minutes on one side, and 2 minutes on the other side.

In buttered ovenproof dish, place sorrel. Lay fish over sorrel. Dot with butter and sprinkle with lemon juice. Bake at 400° F. for 5 minutes. Garnish with halved hard-cooked eggs and slices of lemon.

Serves 4 to 6.

WINE: *A chilled dry white wine:*
Muscadet; Bordeaux Graves; French chablis; Pouilly-Fuissé; white Côtes du Rhône.

CODFISH PROVENÇALE

2 lbs. codfish	1 1-lb.—12-oz. can tomatoes; with liquid
2 tablesp. oil	1 tablesp. flour
2 medium-size onions, chopped	1 cup dry white wine

Cut fish into slices approximately 1½ inches thick. Heat oil in large, heavy skillet. Add onions and cook until slightly browned. Add fish and cook until fish is golden brown. Remove fish and set aside. Add tomatoes to pan. Sprinkle with flour. Stir in wine and liquid from can of tomatoes. Bring to boil. Return fish to pan and cook, without allowing to boil, for 20 minutes. Serve hot.

Serves 4.

WINE: *A chilled dry white wine:*
Bordeaux Graves; Alsatian Riesling; Pouilly-Fuissé; French chablis; Pinot Blanc.

SALMON ALSATIAN

2 lbs. salmon, skinned	1 teasp. salt
2 cups Alsatian Riesling wine	1/2 teasp. pepper
	2 tablesp. butter
2 cups water	4 cups cooked spinach
2 medium-size carrots, sliced	3 tablesp. heavy cream
2 medium-size onions, sliced	3 egg yolks
1 small bay leaf	1 tablesp. flour

Place salmon in heavy saucepan. Add wine, water, carrots, onions, bay leaf, salt, pepper, and 1 tablespoon butter. Bring to boil. Lower flame and simmer for 45 minutes.

Meanwhile, combine spinach and cream. Heat. Stir in yolks and continue cooking over medium flame for 5 minutes. In heated serving dish, arrange spinach in a layer. Cut salmon into slices 1/2 inch thick and arrange slices on spinach bed. Keep warm.

In small saucepan, heat remaining butter. Add flour. Stir in 1/2 cup cooking liquid and cook, stirring, until smooth and thickened. Pour over salmon. Serve hot.

Serves 4 to 6.

Also good for swordfish and tuna fish.

WINE: *A chilled dry white wine:*
Bordeaux Graves; Alsatian Riesling; Pouilly-Fuissé; French chablis; Pinot Blanc.

TROUT IN WINE

1 3-lb. dressed trout*	1 small bay leaf
2 tablesp. chopped scallions (white part only)	pinch of thyme
	½ cup red wine
2 tablesp. chopped parsley	⅛ cup bottled clam juice
1 cup fresh or canned mushrooms, sliced	½ teasp. salt
	¼ teasp. pepper

In buttered heatproof dish, place 1 tablespoon scallions, 1 tablespoon parsley, ½ cup mushrooms, bay leaf, thyme, wine, clam juice, salt, and pepper. Bring to boil and simmer for 5 minutes. Add trout. Cover trout with remaining scallions, parsley, and mushrooms. Dot with butter. Bake at 400° F. for 35 minutes. Serve hot in baking dish with boiled potatoes.

Serves 4.

WINE: *A light red wine:*
Red Bordeaux; domestic claret.

MATELOTE OF EELS

2 lbs. eels, skinned and cut into pieces 1½-inches long	⅛ cup brandy
	2 tablesp. butter
2 medium-size onions, chopped	12 small white onions
	1 cup fresh or canned mushrooms, sliced
1 bay leaf	
pinch of thyme	¼ teasp. pepper
2 sprigs parsley	8 slices French bread, fried in butter
1 clove garlic	
2 cups red wine	1 tablesp. beurre manié
½ teasp. salt	

In large, heavy saucepan, combine eels, chopped onion, bay leaf, thyme, parsley, garlic, wine, and salt. Bring to boil. Add brandy and ignite. Cover and simmer for 15 minutes. Remove eels to heated dish and keep warm.

Meanwhile, in small saucepan, heat 1 tablespoon butter. Add small onions and cook for 10 minutes, or until onions are slightly browned.

Strain cooking liquid from eels and return liquid to pan. Add mushrooms, small onions, and pepper. Bring to

* Or small fresh or frozen trout.

boil and simmer for 10 minutes. Return eels to pan and continue cooking for 10 minutes, or until eels are tender. Add beurre manié. Cook for a few seconds, until sauce thickens. Remove eels to heated serving dish. Surround with onions and mushrooms.

Off fire, add remaining butter cut into small pieces. Pour sauce over eels. Garnish with fried bread. Serve hot.
Serves 4.

WINE: *A light red wine:*
        Red Bordeaux; Beaujolais; domestic claret.
        Or a chilled dry white wine:
        Pouilly-Fuissé; white Côtes du Rhône; Alsatian Riesling; Pinot Blanc.
        Or a rosé wine.

SNAILS

The preparation, cleaning and cooking of snails is such a long and delicate operation that it is preferable to buy canned snails which are ready to cook.

Shells are generally sold separately. They may be washed and re-used.

SNAILS BOURGUIGNONNE

4 dozen snails	2 cloves garlic, crushed
¾ lb. butter	1 teasp. salt
2 teasp. finely chopped onion	¼ teasp. pepper
	⅛ cup bread crumbs
2 tablesp. finely chopped parsley	

In mixing bowl, combine butter, onion, parsley, garlic, salt, and pepper. Mix thoroughly.

In the bottom of each shell put a small quantity of butter mixture. Add snail. Fill shell with butter mixture. Arrange snails, bottom down, on special dish (or baking dish). Sprinkle with bread crumbs. Bake at 400° F. for 8 minutes. Serve very hot.
Serves 4.

WINE: *A chilled dry white wine:*
         Bordeaux Graves; French chablis; Pouilly-Fuissé;
         white Côtes du Rhône.

BOUILLABAISSE

Contrary to "La Marseillaise" (which did not origi-
nate in Marseille but in Strasbourg), "la bouillabaisse" is
a native of Marseille and the favorite child of the whole
Côte d'Azur. It was, and has remained, a fisherman's
meal, and can never be as perfect as a family or restaurant dish—but even so, it is delectable enough to have
won the recognition of gourmets everywhere.

Try it sometime at the beach and you will get the full
flavor of this marvelous dish. The best I have ever eaten
was during a summer vacation I spent with relatives on
the Côte d'Azur, at a small cottage near Toulon. One
time, during the night, or very early in the morning, at
any rate, long before I woke up, the men had left for
fishing. Late in the morning, the women got busy making
the fire on the beach, slicing the bread, preparing the
herbs, etc.

Then the men came back, bringing the fish. The
women became more frantically busy, cleaning the fish,
cutting some into pieces, putting aside some others, and
in no time at all, the bouillabaisse was quickly boiling in
the large copper caldron.

When we ate it, it was so delicious that I have never
forgotten it, and have never tasted any other I found
quite as good. Or perhaps it was the sea, and the sun,
and all the fragrances of summer in a lovely region?

Bouillabaisse is made in France with Mediterranean
fish, which is, of course, not to be found in the United
States. The following recipe lists the equivalent American fish. Even in France, there is no set list of fish—variety
of flavors and textures is more important than any defi-
nite kind.

If some of the fish listed is not available, replace it by
some similar variety.

1 lb. red snapper
1 lb. cod tail
1 lb. bass (striped or sea bass)
2 lobster tails (fresh or frozen)
¾ lb. shrimps, de-veined
1½ lbs. mussels, cleaned but still in the shell
1 lb. eel
1½ lbs. white-meated fish filets
½ cup olive oil
3 tablesp. chopped onion
3 tablesp. tomato paste
2 cloves garlic, crushed
1 bay leaf
pinch of thyme
pinch of dried fennel seeds
pinch of saffron
1 piece dried orange rind
1 teasp. salt
¼ teasp. freshly ground pepper
15 slices French bread, dried in oven (not toasted)
2 tablesp. chopped parsley

Cut fish and lobster into pieces 1½ inches thick. Reserve fish filets. In kettle or large, heavy saucepan, combine oil, onions, tomato paste, garlic, bay leaf, thyme, fennel, saffron, orange rind, shellfish and fish (except filets), salt, pepper, and 6 cups of boiling water. Bring to boil and continue boiling, over brisk flame, for 10 minutes. Add fish filets and continue boiling for 5 minutes longer. Remove all fish and shellfish to heated serving dish and keep warm.

Arrange slices of bread in bottom of soup tureen. Pour cooking liquid over bread. Sprinkle both dishes with parsley. Serve hot. Serve both dishes together.

For eating: serve from both dishes into the same soup plate.

Serves 10 to 12.

WINE: *A chilled dry white wine:*
Bordeaux Graves; Alsatian Riesling; Pouilly-Fuissé; French chablis; Pinot Blanc.

COQUILLES ST. JACQUES

The real Coquilles St. Jacques is not available in this country. What is available are the sea scallops, which may be cooked and served as are the French "Coquilles St. Jacques."

Excellent "Coquilles" may also be made by replacing

the sea scallops by shrimps, shelled and de-veined, but not cooked.

"Coquilles" (shells) are sold by gourmet stores, department stores, mail-order novelty houses, etc. You can buy either the real shells or some lovely fancy ones in ovenproof glass or china. It is well worth the investment because "Coquilles St. Jacques" properly served is an elegant dish, fit for the most formal dinner as a "grand ouverture."

For informal dining, or for Lent, served with a vegetable and a green salad, it is a complete meal, delicate and tasty.

COQUILLES ST. JACQUES PARISIENNE
(Sea Scallops à la Paris)

1½ lbs. sea scallops	1 cup milk
1½ cups dry white wine	¼ cup coarsely chopped
½ teasp. salt	mushrooms
¼ teasp. white pepper	2 tablesp. grated Swiss
3 tablesp. butter	cheese
2 tablesp. flour	2 tablesp. bread crumbs

In large, heavy saucepan, combine scallops, wine, salt, and pepper. Bring slowly to boil and simmer gently for 5 minutes. Drain. Set cooking liquid aside. Cut scallops into small pieces. Meanwhile, in heavy saucepan, heat 2 tablespoons butter. Add flour. Stir in cooking liquid and milk. Cook for 3 minutes, stirring constantly. Add scallops and mushrooms. Cook for 5 minutes, stirring occasionally. Off fire, add Swiss cheese. Mix well. Correct seasoning. Fill buttered shells or individual casseroles with scallop mixture. Sprinkle with bread crumbs. Dot with remaining butter. Broil under broiler flame until top is browned. Serve hot.

Serves 4 to 6.

WINE: *A chilled white wine:*
DRY: Bordeaux Graves; Alsatian Riesling or Traminer; Sauvignon Blanc.
SWEET: Bordeaux Sauternes; Gewurztraminer; sweet Semillon.

COQUILLES ST. JACQUES MENAGERE
(Sea Scallops Home-Style)

1½ lbs. sea scallops	2 tablesp. butter
1½ cups dry white wine	¼ cup mushrooms, finely
½ teasp. salt	chopped
¼ teasp. pepper	1 tablesp. chopped parsley
2 tablesp. finely chopped	1 tablesp. tomato paste
onions	

3 tablesp. fresh bread crumbs

In large, heavy saucepan, combine scallops, wine, salt, and pepper. Bring slowly to boil and simmer gently for 5 minutes. Drain. Set cooking liquid aside for further use. In same saucepan, melt butter. Add onions and cook over low flame for 10 minutes. Add mushrooms, parsley, tomato paste, and 1½ tablespoons of bread crumbs. Bring to boil. Simmer gently for 5 minutes, or until sauce is thick and well blended. Cut scallops into small pieces and return to pan. Fill buttered shells or individual casseroles with scallop mixture. Sprinkle with remaining crumbs. Dot with butter. Broil under broiler flame until top is golden. Serve hot.

Serves 4 to 6.

WINE: *A chilled dry white wine:*
Bordeaux Graves; French chablis; Pouilly-Fuissé; white Côtes du Rhône.

MUSSELS MARINIERE

2 quarts mussels	1 tablesp. finely chopped
¼ teasp. pepper	shallots* (or scallions
2 tablesp. chopped parsley	without tops)
pinch of thyme	1 cup dry white wine
	1 tablesp. beurre manié

Wash and scrub mussels. Place mussels in large saucepan. Add pepper (no salt), 1 tablespoon parsley, thyme,

---

* Shallots stand somewhere between garlic and onions, with a distinctive though subtle flavor of their own. They are small, russet brown, and divided inside into bulblets like garlic. Though somewhat difficult to obtain, the results justify the trouble. A substitute is the white part of the scallion.

shallots (or scallions), and wine. Bring to boil and continue simmering for 8 to 10 minutes, or until the mussel shells open. Discard top shell and keep mussels warm in heated serving dish. Bring cooking liquid to boil in pan and continue boiling for 5 minutes. Add beurre manié. Correct seasoning. Add remaining parsley. Cook for 3 minutes, or until the sauce thickens. Pour over mussels. Serve hot.

Serves 4.

WINE: *A chilled dry white wine:*
Bordeaux Graves; Alsatian Riesling; Pouilly-Fuissé; French chablis; Pinot Blanc.

ROCK LOBSTER A LA BORDELAISE

Originally, this was a recipe (probably the finest) for crawfish. I have the recipe which was given to me by the owner of one of the best restaurants in Bordeaux. It begins with the following words: "First, castrate the crawfish"—and goes into explaining how to perform this delicate operation.

Those few words tell you why crawfish is not a family dish. French housewives are as sensitive as their American sisters when it comes to transforming cooking into some kind of surgery. This is why some of the masterpieces of French cuisine are eaten in restaurants only. But the French cook, with her usual flexibility, has adapted this recipe (and others for crawfish) to rock lobster.

It is equally delicious with fresh or frozen rock lobster. It is one of the very few "grande cuisine" dishes which are easy to prepare and quick to cook. You may serve it in the cooking skillet, if your skillet is good-looking enough. Any way it is served, it looks gorgeous: the bright red of the lobster and the sauce, set off by the green of the parsley, make with the white rice a most appetizing "ensemble."

It deserves to be accompanied by the greatest dry white wine (preferably a Graves) you can afford.

SHRIMPS EN BROCHETTE

1 to 1½ lbs. jumbo shrimps, shelled and de-veined	¼ cup sour cream
	2 tablesp. lemon juice
6 strips bacon, cut into squares	½ teasp. salt
	¼ teasp. pepper

Fill 6 metal skewers with alternating shrimp and bacon. Brush with melted butter. Broil for 4 to 6 minutes 2 to 3 inches from heat, turning the skewers once and basting occasionally with melted butter. Remove to heated serving dish and keep warm.

In small saucepan, heat sour cream over low flame. Add lemon juice and juice from broiled shrimps. Cook over low flame for 5 minutes. Season with salt and pepper. Pour over shrimps. Serve hot.

Serves 6.

WINE: *A chilled white wine:*
DRY: Bordeaux Graves; Alsatian Riesling or Traminer; Sauvignon Blanc.
SWEET: Bordeaux Sauternes; Gewurztraminer; sweet Semillon.

FRIED FROGS' LEGS

2 lbs. frogs' legs, skinned and trimmed	1 tablesp. chopped parsley
	½ clove garlic, crushed
½ teasp. salt	fritter batter
¼ teasp. pepper	oil for frying
2 tablesp. lemon juice	fried parsley
2 tablesp. vegetable oil	

In deep bowl, combine frogs' legs, salt, pepper, lemon juice, oil, parsley, and garlic. Let stand for 1 hour. Dry legs with paper towels. Dip in fritter batter and deep-fry until well browned. Drain. Garnish with fried parsley.

Serves 4.

WINE: *A chilled dry white wine:*
Bordeaux Graves; French chablis; Pouilly-Fuissé; white Côtes du Rhône.

Chapter VI

Poultry

CHICKEN MARENGO

A T THE END of the Eighteenth century, under the Directoire, there opened in Paris a restaurant called "Les Trois Frères Provençaux" ("the Three Provençal Brothers") which was owned, as could be expected from the name, by three brothers who came from the Provence region.

The restaurant, located in the Palais-Royal, the heart of the French Revolution, became famous overnight. The addition of spicy ingredients to Parisian cooking was a revelation to the patrons. Members of the Directoire and the Assemblies, army suppliers, even "nouveaux riches" and lovely ladies "de peu de vertu," crowded the new restaurant.

The Provençal brothers were among the few great cooks and gourmets who at that time restored French cuisine, nearly killed by the "Spartan brew" of the Jacobins, to a high degree of excellence.

They created many dishes which are now part of everyday cooking. One of the best liked is chicken (or veal) Marengo. It was so named in honor of the victory the then General Napoleon Bonaparte won during his campaign of Italy.

1 2½-to-3-lb. ready-to-cook broiler, quartered	1 clove garlic, crushed
2 tablesp. salad oil	¼ teasp. thyme
2 medium-size onions, chopped	1 bay leaf
1 tablesp. flour	½ teasp. salt
½ cup consommé	¼ teasp. pepper
¼ cup dry white wine	½ lb. mushrooms, sliced
3 tablesp. tomato paste	1 tablesp. chopped parsley
	4 slices French bread, fried in butter

In a large, heavy skillet, cook chicken in heated oil until browned on both sides. Add onions, and cook until onions are slightly browned. Sprinkle with flour, and cook for 3 minutes, stirring constantly. Add consommé, wine, tomato paste, garlic, thyme, bay leaf, salt, and pepper. Bring to boil. Cover and simmer gently for 30 minutes, or until meat is tender. Remove chicken to heated serving dish and keep warm. Add mushrooms to skillet. Cover and cook over low flame for 15 minutes. Pour over chicken. Sprinkle with parsley. Garnish with slices of fried bread.

Serves 4.

WINE: *A full-bodied red wine:*
       French red Bordeaux; French red Burgundy; red Côtes du Rhône; domestic claret or Burgundy; Pinot Noir; Cabernet.

COQ AU VIN
(Chicken with Wine)

1 2½-to-3-lb. broiler, quartered	1 clove garlic, crushed
2 tablesp. oil	1 bay leaf
1 tablesp. chopped onion	¼ teaspoon thyme
1 tablesp. flour	12 small white onions
½ cup red wine	1 cup mushrooms, sliced
½ cup clear chicken broth	4 slices French bread, fried in butter

In a large, heavy skillet, cook chicken and chopped onion in heated oil until slightly browned. Stir in flour and cook until well browned. Add wine, chicken broth, garlic, bay leaf, thyme, white onions, and mushrooms. Bring to boil. Cover. Simmer for 45 minutes, or until meat is tender. Garnish with slices of fried bread.

Serves 4.

Serve with boiled potatoes.

WINE: *A full-bodied red wine:*
French red Bordeaux; French red Burgundy; red Côtes du Rhône; domestic claret or Burgundy; Pinot Noir; Cabernet.

CHICKEN WITH TARRAGON

1 tablesp. butter	3 cups clear chicken broth
2 medium-size carrots, sliced	3 cups water
1 medium-size onion, sliced	½ teasp. dried tarragon
2 sprigs green celery tops	leaves
4 sprigs parsley	1 clove
1 2½-to-3-lb. ready-to-cook	½ tablesp. salt
chicken	2 egg yolks

Melt butter in Dutch oven. Add carrots, onions, celery, and parsley. Cover and cook over low flame for 30 minutes. Lay chicken over vegetables. Add chicken broth and water. Bring to boil. Add ¼ teaspoon tarragon, clove, and salt. Cover and simmer very gently for 1½ hours, or until chicken is tender. Keep warm.

In small, heavy saucepan, place 3 cups of liquid in which chicken was cooked, and add ¼ teaspoon tarragon. Bring to boil over brisk flame until reduced to half. Stir in egg yolks and heat without boiling.

Serve chicken on a heated platter. Serve sauce in sauce boat.

Serves 4.

Serve with rice.

WINE: *A light red wine:*
Red Bordeaux; Beaujolais; domestic claret.
Or a chilled white wine:

Pouilly-Fuissé; white Côtes du Rhône; Alsatian
Riesling; Pinot Blanc.
Or a rosé wine.

FRICASSEE OF CHICKEN

1 2½-to-3-lb. broiler, quartered	1 teasp. salt
2 tablesp. butter	2 sprigs parsley
1 tablesp. flour	1 small bay leaf
2 cups warm water	pinch of thyme
1 onion, studded with one clove	¼ teasp. pepper
	2 egg yolks
	2 tablesp. heavy cream

In chicken fryer, heat butter. Add chicken. Cover and
cook over medium flame for 10 minutes (do not let meat
brown). Sprinkle with flour. Add water and bring to
boil, stirring constantly. Add onion, parsley, bay leaf,
thyme, salt, and pepper. Cover and simmer for 45 minutes, or until meat is tender. Discard onion, parsley, and
bay leaf. Remove chicken to heated serving dish and keep
warm. Blend sauce with egg yolks and cream. Pour over
meat. Serve hot.

Serves 4.

Serve with rice or boiled potatoes.

WINE: *A light red wine:*
        Red Bordeaux; Beaujolais; domestic claret.
        Or a chilled dry white wine:
        Pouilly-Fuissé; white Côtes du Rhône; Alsatian
        Riesling; Pinot Blanc.
        Or a rosé wine.

CHICKEN AU GRATIN

1 2½-to-3-lb. broiler	1 onion, studded with one clove
6 cups water	2 tablesp. heavy cream
1 tablesp. salt	4 cups cooked rice, kept warm
1 bay leaf	3 egg yolks
pinch of thyme	2 tablesp. grated Swiss cheese
2 sprigs parsley	
4 peppercorns	
1 stalk celery	

In Dutch oven, combine water, salt, bay leaf, thyme, parsley, peppercorns, celery, and onion. Bring to boil. Add chicken. Bring again to boil. Cover and simmer gently 1½ hours, or until meat is very tender. Remove chicken and bone it. Reserve 1 cup cooking liquid.

Place rice in heated ovenproof casserole. Arrange chicken on top of rice. Keep warm.

In small, heavy saucepan, cook reserved cooking liquid. Bring to boil. Blend sauce with egg yolks. Off fire, add cheese. Mix well. Pour over meat. Dot with butter. Broil under broiler flame until top is well browned.

Serves 4.

WINE: *A light red wine:*
Red Bordeaux; Beaujolais; domestic claret.
Or a chilled dry white wine:
Pouilly-Fuissé; white Côtes du Rhône; Alsatian Riesling or Traminer; Pinot Blanc.
Or a rosé wine.

CHICKEN OF THE DUKES

1 3-to-4-lb. ready-to-cook chicken, quartered
¼ cup butter
3 medium-size onions, chopped fine
1 tablesp. salt
¼ teasp. freshly ground pepper
1 tablesp. flour
1 cup scalded milk
pinch of grated nutmeg
2 tablesp. Armagnac (or other brandy)
⅛ cup heavy cream
2 tablesp. Madeira wine
1 tablesp. lemon juice

In chicken fryer, heat 1 tablespoon butter. Add onions. Cover and cook over very low flame for 10 minutes. Remove onions and set aside. To same pan, add 2 tablespoons butter. Heat butter. Add chicken and cook over low flame for 10 minutes. Return onions to pan. Add salt and pepper. Cover and cook over low flame for 40 minutes, or until chicken is tender.

Meanwhile, heat remaining butter in small, heavy saucepan. Add flour. Stir in milk. Add salt to taste, and nutmeg. Bring to boil, stirring constantly. Simmer for 10 minutes.

Remove chicken to heated serving dish and keep warm. Add Armagnac (or other brandy) to pan. Bring to boil. Add sauce from saucepan, and heavy cream. Bring to boil and cook for 5 minutes, stirring constantly. Off fire, add Madeira wine and lemon juice. Correct seasoning. Serve hot.

Serves 4.

WINE: *A light red wine:*
Red Bordeaux; Beaujolais; domestic claret.
Or a chilled dry white wine:
Pouilly-Fuissé; white Côtes du Rhône; Alsatian Riesling; Pinot Blanc.
Or a rosé wine.

CHICKEN TOURAINE

1 2-to-3-lb. broiler, quartered
2 tablesp. butter
12 small white onions, whole
½ cup fresh or canned mushrooms, sliced
½ cup canned tomatoes, drained and crushed
½ cup sweet white wine
1 teasp. salt
¼ teasp. freshly ground pepper
½ teasp. paprika
½ cup sour cream

In chicken fryer, heat butter. Add chicken and cook until lightly browned on both sides. Add onions, and continue cooking until onions are well browned. Add mushrooms, tomatoes, wine, salt, pepper, and paprika. Bring to boil. Cover and simmer for 45 minutes, or until chicken is tender. Remove chicken to heated serving dish and keep warm. Add sour cream to pan and heat, stirring constantly, without allowing to boil. Pour over chicken. Serve hot.

Serves 4.

WINE: *A full-bodied red wine:*
French red Bordeaux; French red Burgundy; red Côtes du Rhône; domestic claret or Burgundy.

CHICKEN DIJON

Dijon is the capital of Burgundy and has made a name for itself with the famed "Dijon mustard"—so it is no surprise to find a recipe from there using wine and mustard.

1 2½-to-3-lb. broiler, quartered	½ teasp. salt
2 tablesp. butter	¼ teasp. pepper
2 cups dry white wine	2 egg yolks
¼ teasp. dried tarragon leaves	2 tablesp. prepared mustard (Dijon style)
pinch of thyme	2 tablesp. sour cream
1 small bay leaf	pinch of cayenne pepper

In chicken fryer, heat butter. Add chicken and cook until chicken is well browned on both sides. Add wine, tarragon, thyme, bay leaf, salt, and pepper. Bring to boil. Cover and simmer for 45 minutes, or until meat is tender. Remove meat to heated serving dish and keep warm.

Discard bay leaf. Blend sauce with egg yolks. Add sour cream, mustard, and cayenne pepper. Heat, stirring briskly and constantly. Do not allow to boil. Pour over chicken.

Serves 4.

WINE: *A chilled dry white wine:*
Muscadet; Bordeaux Graves; French chablis; Pouilly-Fuissé; white Côtes du Rhône.

CHICKEN BORDEAUX

1 2½-to-3-lb. broiler, quartered	2 tablesp. flour
¼ cup flour	1½ teasp. sugar
1 teasp. salt	1 cup dry white Bordeaux wine
¼ teasp. pepper	½ cup fresh or canned mushrooms, sliced
¼ cup vegetable oil	
½ cup canned tomatoes	

Dredge chicken with flour. Salt with ½ teaspoon salt. Pepper.

In chicken fryer, heat oil. Add chicken and cook until

well browned on both sides. Cover and cook over low heat for 25 minutes.

Combine tomatoes, 2 tablespoons flour, sugar, and remaining salt. Add tomato mixture to pan. Add wine and mushrooms. Cover and continue cooking over low flame for 20 minutes, or until chicken is tender. Serve hot.

Serves 4.

WINE: *A light red wine:*
Red Bordeaux; Beaujolais; domestic claret.
Or a chilled dry white wine:
Bordeaux Graves; Pouilly-Fuissé; white Côtes du Rhône; Alsatian Riesling; Pinot Blanc.
Or a rosé wine.

POULET EN COCOTE
(Chicken Cocote)

Basically, chicken cocote is a chicken which has first been browned in butter and then slowly cooked in the oven with a garnish of diced vegetables. Sliced mushrooms may be substituted for artichokes. Mixed vegetables (carrots, celery, string beans, etc.) go equally well with it.

¼ lb. salt pork, cut into half-inch dice	1 lb. potatoes, diced
2 tablesp. butter	4 artichoke hearts, quartered
12 small white onions	½ teasp. salt
1 2½-to-3-lb. ready-to-cook broiler, whole	¼ teasp. pepper
	¼ cup clear chicken broth
	2 tablesp. consommé

In boiling water, cook pork and onions for 5 minutes. Drain. In heavy skillet, cook pork and onions in heated butter until slightly browned. Remove pork and onions from skillet and set aside. Add chicken to fat in skillet and cook until well browned on all sides. Remove chicken to heated ovenproof casserole. Add pork, onions, potatoes, artichokes, salt, pepper, and chicken broth. Cover and bake at 350° F. for 1½ hours, or until chicken is tender.

Sprinkle chicken with consommé. Serve in casserole.
Carve chicken at the table.

Serves 4.

WINE: *A light red wine:*
Red Bordeaux; Beaujolais; domestic claret.
Or a chilled dry white wine:
Bordeaux Graves; Pouilly-Fuissé; white Côtes du
Rhône; Alsatian Riesling; Pinot Blanc.
Or a rosé wine.

TURKEY STUFFED WITH CHESTNUTS

It is true that there is no Thanksgiving in France, but
there also turkeys are the victims of a "sacrificial rite."

Everybody who can afford it has turkey for the two
"réveillons." "Réveillon de Noël" and "Réveillon du Jour
de l'An" are the dinner-suppers served at midnight the
24th and the 31st of December.

France being mostly a Catholic country, it is traditional to go to midnight mass the night before Christmas.
A very light snack is eaten at dinnertime and, then, when
they come back from church at midnight, the whole family (and friends) sit down at a sumptuous meal. It lasts,
and lasts, and lasts. Whether the meal takes place at
home or in a restaurant, there is much eating, drinking,
dancing, and merry-making.

For the St. Sylvester's "réveillon" (the night before
New Year), the rejoicing goes along the same lines, with
the exception that there is no church-going before the
supper.

In both celebrations, "Dinde aux marrons" (turkey
stuffed with chestnuts) is the highlight of the dinner—
and justly so, because even people who don't as a rule
care much for turkey love it that way.

Served with braised celery and accompanied by a great
Bordeaux, it is truly magnificent.

DINDE AUX MARRONS
(Turkey Stuffed with Chestnuts)

1 8-to-10-lb. ready-to-cook turkey	1 lb. lean pork, ground
2 lbs. chestnuts	1 tablesp. salt
2 cups consommé	¼ teasp. pepper
1 cup water	⅛ cup brandy
2 lbs. sausage meat	4 thin slices salt pork

With a sharp kitchen knife, cut an incision through the shell of each chestnut. Place chestnuts on cookie sheet and bake at 450° F. for 10 minutes. Shell chestnuts.

In large saucepan, combine chestnuts, consommé, and water. Bring to boil. Cover and simmer for 20 minutes. Drain and let cool.

In mixing bowl, combine chestnuts, sausage meat, ground pork, salt, pepper, and brandy. Mix thoroughly.

Stuff bird with chestnut mixture. Sew up the opening. Cover breast of turkey with slices of salt pork. Cover with buttered wax paper. Place on rack in roasting pan. Pour 3 tablespoons water in pan. Roast at 450° for 15 minutes. Reduce oven temperature to 375° and continue roasting for 1 hour. Remove wax paper. Continue roasting for 30 minutes. Remove salt pork and continue roasting for 2½ hours, or until well done, turning bird in order to brown all sides, and basting occasionally with fat from pan. For the last half-hour, let bird stand breast-side up.

For gravy: Pour off excess fat from cooking liquid in pan. Add ¼ cup boiling water and bringing to boil, scraping bottom of pan until all brown crust is entirely dissolved. Do not thicken. Correct seasoning.

WINE: A great Bordeaux or a great French Burgundy.

SQUABS WITH PEAS

3 ready-to-cook squabs	¼ lb. salt pork, diced
2 tablesp. butter	1 tablesp. flour
12 small white onions	1 cup clear chicken broth
2 cups peas (fresh or canned)	

In Dutch oven or heavy saucepan, heat 1 tablespoon butter. Add squabs, onions, and salt pork, and cook until squabs are well browned on all sides. Remove squabs, onions, and salt pork and set aside. Pour fat off pan. Add remaining butter to pan. Heat butter. Add flour and cook until slightly browned. Stir in chicken broth. Return to pan squabs, onions, and salt pork. Add peas. Bring to boil. Cover and simmer for 30 minutes. Serve hot.

(If canned peas are used, add peas to pan 5 minutes before end of cooking time.)

Serves 4.

WINE: *A light red wine:*
        Red Bordeaux; Beaujolais; domestic claret.
        Or a chilled dry white wine:
        Bordeaux Graves; Pouilly-Fuissé; white Côtes du Rhône; Alsatian Riesling; Pinot Blanc.
        Or a rosé wine.

SQUABS ON CANAPES

4 ready-to-cook squabs
4 thin slices salt pork
¼ cup melted butter
¼ cup dry white wine
½ teasp. salt
¼ teasp. pepper
4 slices French bread, fried in butter
1 tablesp. butter

Place a slice of salt pork on breast of each squab. Place squabs in roasting pan. In a bowl combine melted butter and wine. Roast squabs at 400° F., basting frequently with butter mixture, for 30 minutes, or until meat is tender. Discard salt pork. Season with salt and pepper.

Meanwhile, chop squab livers. In a small skillet, heat butter. Add livers, and cook over brisk flame for 5 minutes, or until browned.

Place slices of fried bread on heated serving dish and keep warm. Spread bread with cooked liver. Place a squab on each slice. Serve hot.

Serves 4.

Serve with potato chips.

WINE: *A light red wine:*
Red Bordeaux; Beaujolais; domestic claret.
Or a chilled dry white wine:
Pouilly-Fuissé; white Côtes du Rhône; Alsatian
Riesling; Pinot Blanc.
Or a rosé wine.

DUCKLING WITH PEAS

1 5-to-6-lb. ready-to-cook duckling	4 leaves lettuce
1 tablesp. butter	1 small bay leaf
¼ lb. salt pork, diced	pinch of thyme
12 small white onions	2 sprigs parsley
1 tablesp. flour	½ teasp. salt
1 cup consommé	¼ teasp. pepper
3 cups fresh (or canned) peas	

In large saucepan, heat butter. Add salt pork and cook
until slightly browned. Add onions and cook until well
browned. Remove salt pork and onions and set aside.
Add duckling to pan, and cook until well browned on all
sides. Remove duckling and set aside. Pour off fat, keeping only 1 tablespoon of fat in pan. Add flour to pan
and cook until well browned. Stir in consommé. Return
salt pork, onions, and duckling to pan. Add peas, lettuce
leaves, bay leaf, thyme, parsley, salt, and pepper. Bring
to boil. Cover and simmer for 1 hour, or until meat is
tender.

For serving: Carve duckling and arrange on heated
serving dish. Surround with peas. Serve hot.

Serves 4 to 6.

WINE: *A light red wine:*
Red Bordeaux; Beaujolais; domestic claret.
Or a chilled dry white wine:
Pouilly-Fuissé; white Côtes du Rhône; Alsatian
Riesling; Pinot Blanc.
Or a rosé wine.

DUCKLING WITH OLIVES

1 5-to-6-lb. ready-to-cook duckling	1 bay leaf
1 tablesp. butter	pinch of thyme
1 tablesp. flour	2 sprigs parsley
1 cup consommé	½ teasp. salt
	¼ teasp. pepper
36 green olives, pitted	

In large saucepan, heat butter. Add duckling and cook until well browned on all sides. Remove duckling and set aside. Pour fat off pan, leaving only 1 tablespoon of fat. Add flour, and cook until flour is well browned. Stir in consommé. Add bay leaf, thyme, parsley, salt, and pepper. Return duckling to pan. Bring to boil. Cover and simmer for 1 hour, or until meat is tender. Remove duckling to heated serving dish. Carve and arrange.

Meanwhile, cook olives for 5 minutes in boiling water. Drain. Add to pan. Cook 5 minutes. Pour olive sauce over meat. Serve hot.

Serves 4 to 6.

WINE: *A chilled dry white wine:*
> Bordeaux Graves; Alsatian Riesling; Pouilly-Fuissé; French chablis; Pinot Blanc.

DUCK A L'ORANGE

This is the family version of the classic duck à l'orange. It is surprisingly simple when compared to the classic one, and tastes just as good.

1 3½-to-4-lb duckling, quartered	1 tablesp. flour
⅓ cup orange marmalade	¾ cup dry white wine
1 tablesp. soy sauce	1 tablesp. wine vinegar
1 teasp. salt	¼ cup consommé
1 tablesp butter	¼ teasp. pepper
	1 orange, peeled and cut into wedges

In mixing bowl, combine marmalade, soy sauce, and salt. Roast duckling at 450° F. for 15 minutes. Reduce heat to 400° and continue roasting, brushing occasionally with half of orange mixture, for 30 minutes, or until meat is tender. Meanwhile, heat butter in a small sauce-pan. Add flour and cook until flour is browned. Stir in wine, vinegar, and consommé. Bring to boil, stirring constantly. Cover and simmer for 10 minutes. Add remaining orange mixture. Cover and continue simmering for 10 minutes more. Add pepper.

Meanwhile, cook orange wedges in boiling water for 3 minutes. Drain. Keep warm.

Remove duckling to heated serving dish and keep warm. Pour excess fat off duckling pan. Add remaining cooking liquid to saucepan in which orange sauce is cooking. Mix. For serving: garnish with wedges of orange. Serve sauce in sauceboat. Serve hot.

Serves 4.

Serve with matchstick potatoes.

WINE: *A light red wine:*
         Red Bordeaux; Beaujolais; domestic claret.
         Or a chilled dry wine:
         Bordeaux Graves; Pouilly-Fuissé; white Côtes du
         Rhône; Alsatian Riesling; Pinot Blanc.
         Or a rosé wine.

GUINEA HEN "FORESTERS"

1 tablesp. butter	1 lb. potatoes, diced
¼ lb. salt pork, diced	½ cup clear chicken broth
12 small white onions	¼ teasp. salt
2 2-to-2½-lb. ready-to-cook	pinch of pepper
guinea hens	1 tablesp. vegetable oil
1 cup fresh or canned mushrooms, sliced	

In heatproof casserole, heat butter. Add salt pork and onions, and cook until slightly browned. Remove salt pork and onions and set aside. Add guinea hens to pan. Cook for 10 minutes, or until well browned on all sides. Return onions and salt pork to pan. Add potatoes, chicken broth, salt, and pepper. Bake at 400° F. for 30 minutes, or until meat is tender.

Meanwhile, in small saucepan, heat oil. Add mushrooms and cook for 10 minutes. Add mushroom to guinea hen casserole, just before serving.

Serve hot.

Serves 4.

WINE: *A light red wine:*
Red Bordeaux; Beaujolais; domestic claret.
Or a chilled dry white wine:
Bordeaux Graves; Pouilly-Fuissé; white Côtes du
Rhône; Alsatian Riesling; Pinot Blanc.
Or a rosé wine.

PHEASANT NORMANDY

1 pheasant, cleaned and trussed	½ cup sour cream
2 thin slices salt pork	1 teasp. salt
2 tablesp. butter	¼ teasp. freshly ground pepper
6 apples, peeled and sliced	⅛ cup applejack

Place slices of salt pork on breast of pheasant. Tie with
string. In heatproof casserole, heat butter. Place pheasant in casserole and cook until well browned on all sides.
Cover and simmer for 15 minutes. Add apples, sour
cream, salt, and pepper. Stir in applejack. Bring to boiling point but do not allow to boil. Cover and simmer for
30 minutes, or until meat is tender. Discard string. Serve
hot in casserole.

Serves 3 to 4.

WINE: *A light red wine:*
Red Bordeaux; Beaujolais; domestic claret.
Or a chilled dry wine:
Pouilly-Fuissé; white Côtes du Rhône; Alsatian
Riesling; Pinot Blanc.
Or a rosé wine.

Chapter VII

Meat

BEEF BOURGUIGNON

Beef Bourguinon is one of the famous French dishes that you can eat all over the world, but probably the best you can eat anywhere is the one you can make at home.

The meat is always cooked until it is fork-tender, and the sauce is always tasty. This is usually enough for most restaurants and, except for a few top ones, they simplify the recipe and make do with second-choice ingredients. Beef Bourguignon is so delectable in itself that, even so, it is not bad, but it is not as delicious as when it is carefully home-made.

The meat may be cooked either in one piece (and then sliced for serving), or cut into cubes. The latter is generally preferred because the meat is tastier.

Beef Bourguignon is never prepared in small quantity. The right proportions are for 6 to 8 persons. Prepare it for a party dinner (kept warm in a chafing dish it makes a wonderful buffet dish), or for two family meals. It is better when reheated. It may also be frozen and kept in the freezer.

3 lbs. chuck or top round of beef, cut into 2-inch cubes
1 small onion, sliced
2 cups red wine
1 small bay leaf
4 sprigs parsley
pinch of thyme
2 tablesp. salad oil
½ teasp. salt
¼ teasp. pepper
1 small carrot, sliced
1 clove garlic, crushed
3 tablesp. butter
1 tablesp. flour
½ cup consommé
¼ lb. salt pork, diced
24 small white onions
1 cup fresh or canned mushrooms, sliced

In deep bowl, combine meat, sliced onion, wine, bay leaf, parsley, thyme, oil, salt, pepper, carrot, and garlic. Let stand for 4 hours, turning meat occasionally. Remove meat and pat dry with paper towels. Strain marinade and set aside for further use.

In Dutch oven or large, heavy saucepan, heat 2 tablespoons butter. Add meat and cook until well browned on all sides. Add flour and cook for 3 minutes, stirring constantly. Stir in consommé and marinade. Bring to boil. Cover and simmer for 2 hours. Meanwhile, in a small saucepan, heat remaining butter. Add salt pork and onions, and cook over medium flame for 10 minutes, or until pork and onions are golden brown. Remove them to pan in which meat is cooking. Add mushrooms. Bring to boil. Cover and simmer for 45 minutes, or until meat is fork-tender. Serve hot.

Serves 6 to 8.

Serve with boiled potatoes. Also good with all kinds of macaroni.

WINE: *A red wine:*
        Red Bordeaux; French red Burgundy; red Côtes du Rhône; domestic claret or Burgundy.

BOEUF A LA MODE

Boeuf à la mode is one of the basic dishes of French cuisine. It is served everywhere in France, from the most elegant homes and restaurants to the farmer's table.

Although it is a family dish, it is considered fit for a king, and Marcel Proust, one of the most sophisticated French writers, has written in *Remembrance of Things Past* a lengthy and loving description of boeuf à la mode and the mysterious ways the family cook had of making this dish *the* dish to be anticipated, tasted, and talked about.

Boeuf à la mode is equally good when reheated, and delicious when eaten cold, covered with the jellied sauce.

3 lbs. boneless pot roast	1 lump sugar
2 tablesp. butter	pinch of thyme
4 thin slices of salt pork, cut into small pieces	1 bay leaf
	3 sprigs parsley
12 small white onions	1 teasp. salt
⅛ cup brandy	½ teasp. pepper
1 calf's foot, or veal knuckle	1 cup consommé
3 carrots, cut into 1-inch pieces	1 cup dry white wine

Have the butcher lard the meat. In Dutch oven or large heavy saucepan, heat butter. Add meat and cook over brisk flame until slightly browned on all sides. Add salt pork and onions and continue cooking until well browned. Add brandy and ignite. Add calf's foot, carrots, sugar, thyme, bay leaf, parsley, salt, pepper, consommé, and wine. Bring to boil. Cover tightly and simmer for 4 hours, or until meat is tender. Remove meat and cut it against the grain into thin slices. Arrange slices on heated serving dish. Garnish with onions, carrots, and meat of calf's foot. Skim fat from gravy. Pour a few spoonfuls of gravy on slices of meat. Strain remaining gravy and serve in a sauce boat.

Serves 6.

Serve with boiled potatoes.

WINE: *A full-bodied red wine:*
French red Bordeaux; French red Burgundy; red Côtes du Rhône; domestic claret or Burgundy; Pinot Noir; Cabernet.

CARBONADE
(Beef and Onion Stew)

Carbonade is a specialty of Northern France, where the climate is rough, and where beer is as common as wine is in the rest of France. Hence, Carbonade, a wonderful dish, made with beer.

The recipe sounds like rather coarse fare. Such a large quantity of onions and beer does not seem to be choice ingredients for a fine dish. But perhaps this is a good opportunity to point out an important feature of French cooking: no matter what the ingredients are, once cooked, the flavor of the dish should be delicate. Therefore, the strong flavor of onions never stands out in any preparation.

There is nothing mysterious about the way to prevent this taste from pervading the whole dish. Onions are always cooked in shortening until they are either slightly or well browned, and then they are slowly cooked for a long time. The browning evaporates the pungent flavor, and the slow cooking reduces the onions to a kind of purée, delectable to eat and easy to digest.

3 lbs. boneless pot roast, cut into slices ½-inch thick	1 teasp. granulated sugar
	¼ cup consommé
2 tablesp. butter	1 cup light beer
6 medium-size onions, chopped	½ teasp. salt
	¼ teasp. pepper
½ teasp. flour	1 bay leaf

In Dutch oven or large, heavy saucepan, heat butter. Add meat and cook until well browned on both sides. Remove meat and set aside. Add onions to pan and cook until slightly browned. Stir in flour and sugar and cook until well browned. Stir in consommé and beer. Bring to boil. Return meat to pan. Add salt, pepper, and bay leaf. Cover tightly and simmer for 3 hours, or until meat is tender. Serve hot.

Serves 6.

Serve with noodles or boiled potatoes.

DRINK: *beer*.

BEEF ESTOUFFADE

2 lbs. round of beef	1 cup red wine
3 medium-size carrots, sliced	4 strips bacon, cut into
2 medium-size onions, thinly	small pieces
sliced	1 calf's foot, or calf's knuckle
½ teasp. salt	1 cup consommé
¼ teasp. pepper	4 tomatoes, peeled and
pinch of thyme	quartered
1 bay leaf	16 green pitted olives
2 cloves	1 tablesp. arrowroot

Cut beef into 2-inch cubes. In a bowl, combine meat, carrots, onions, salt, pepper, thyme, bay leaf, cloves, and wine. Let stand for 12 hours, turning meat occasionally. Dry meat with paper towels. Drain marinade. Place vegetables from marinade in a cheesecloth bag tied with a string. In Dutch oven or large, heavy saucepan, place bacon and cook over low flame for 5 minutes. Remove bacon and set aside. Raise flame under the pan. When fat is hot, add meat and cook until well browned on all sides. Lower flame. Cover and simmer for 20 minutes. Add calf's foot, bag of vegetables, consommé, marinade, and tomatoes. Return bacon to pan. Bring to boil. Cover tightly and simmer for 3 hours.

Meanwhile, cook olives in boiling water for 5 minutes. Drain. Cut beef into thin slices. Arrange slices on heated serving dish and keep warm. Bone the calf's foot and dice the meat. Remove meat to serving dish. Add olives, and arrowroot dissolved in water to pan. Cook for 5 minutes. Pour over meat.

Serves 4 to 6.

WINE: *A full-bodied red wine:*
French red Bordeaux; French red Burgundy; red Côtes du Rhône; domestic claret or Burgundy; Pinot Noir; Cabernet.

BEEF ARLESIENNE

3 lbs. boneless pot roast, cut
into slices ½ inch thick
2 tablesp. oil
6 tomatoes, peeled and
quartered
1 4-oz. can sliced mushrooms
and juice
½ cup pitted black olives
1 clove garlic, crushed
½ teasp. salt
¼ teasp. pepper
pinch of dried sweet basil
1 bay leaf

In Dutch oven or large, heavy saucepan, heat oil. Add
meat and cook until well browned on both sides. Pour
fat off pan. Add to pan, tomatoes, mushrooms and juice,
olives, garlic, salt, pepper, basil, and bay leaf. Bring to
boil. Cover tightly and simmer for 3 hours, or until meat
is tender. Serve hot.

Serves 6.

Serve with macaroni.

WINE: *A full-bodied red wine:*
French red Bordeaux; French red Burgundy; red
Côtes du Rhône; domestic claret or Burgundy;
Pinot Noir; Cabernet.

BEEF "EN DAUBE"

2 lbs. boneless pot roast,
larded
4 thin slices salt pork
2 medium-size onions, sliced
2 medium-size carrots, cut
into 1-inch pieces
1 bay leaf
pinch of thyme
½ teasp. salt
¼ teasp. pepper
2 cups red wine
2 tablesp. tomato paste

Line bottom of Dutch oven or large, heavy saucepan
with slices of salt pork. Add onions, carrots, bay leaf,
and thyme. Place meat on vegetable bed. Add salt, pepper, and wine. Bring to boil. Cover and simmer for 3
hours, or until meat is tender.

Remove meat and cut into thin slices. Arrange slices

on heated serving dish and keep warm. Surround with carrots and onions from pan. Add tomato paste to pan. Stir until well blended, and simmer for 5 minutes. Pour over meat. Serve hot. Good when reheated.

Serves 4 to 6.

Serve with boiled potatoes or macaroni.

WINE: *A full-bodied red wine:*
French red Bordeaux; French red Burgundy; red Côtes du Rhône; domestic claret or Burgundy; Pinot Noir; Cabernet.

BRAISED FILET OF BEEF

2 lbs. filet of beef, larded	½ teasp. salt
4 thin slices salt pork	¼ teasp. pepper
¾ cup consommé	1 teasp. arrowroot, dissolved
2 tablesp. brandy	in water

Line the bottom of a heavy saucepan, just large enough to contain the meat, with slices of salt pork. Add meat. Add ¼ cup consommé and brandy. Cook, uncovered, over brisk flame, basting frequently with liquid from pan, for 8 minutes, or until liquid is reduced to approximately 1 tablespoon. Add remaining consommé, salt, and pepper. Bring to boil. Cover and simmer for 45 minutes, basting occasionally with liquid from pan.

Remove meat to heated ovenproof serving dish. Sprinkle meat with 3 tablespoons cooking liquid and bake at 450° F. for 8 minutes. Meanwhile, bring to boil sauce in pan. Add arrowroot dissolved in water, and cook, stirring constantly, for a few seconds, or until sauce is thickened. Serve sauce in sauce boat. Serve hot.

Serves 4 to 6.

WINE: *A full-bodied red wine:*
French red Bordeaux; French red Burgundy; red Côtes du Rhône; domestic claret or Burgundy; Pinot Noir; Cabernet.

BOEUF EN MIROTON
(Beef Miroton)

1 lb. leftover beef	¼ teasp. pepper
2 tablesp. butter	1 tablesp. vinegar
½ lb. onions, finely chopped	5 medium-size boiled
1 tablesp. flour	potatoes
½ cup consommé	2 tablesp. fresh bread
½ teasp. salt	crumbs

In a skillet, heat 1 tablespoon butter. Add onions and cook until slightly browned. Sprinkle with flour and cook until browned, stirring constantly. Stir in consommé, salt, pepper, and vinegar. Bring to boil. Cover and cook over a low flame for 25 minutes.

Meanwhile, cut potatoes into slices about ½ inch thick. Butter an ovenproof casserole and arrange potatoes in crown, each slice overlapping another.

Cut meat into thin slices. Place meat in center of potato crown. Pour onion mixture over meat. Sprinkle with bread crumbs and dot with remaining butter. Bake at 450° F. for 10 minutes.

Serves 4.

WINE: *A red wine:*
Red Bordeaux; French red Burgundy; red Côtes du Rhône; domestic claret or Burgundy.

FRENCH HAMBURGER

They also have it! It is not called hamburger but "Bitoque."

It is different from the American hamburger, but evidently belongs to the same family. Like its American cousin, French hamburger is inexpensive, quickly cooked, and good to eat.

2 lbs. ground beef	¼ teasp. pepper
⅓ cup fresh bread crumbs	¼ cup flour
⅛ cup milk	3 tablesp. butter
½ teasp. salt	3 tablesp. sour cream
	3 tablesp. consommé

Soak crumbs in milk. Squeeze crumbs to remove excess milk. In bowl, combine moistened crumbs, ground beef, salt, and pepper. Mix well. Form mixture into 6 flat patties. Dredge with flour.

In large skillet, heat butter. Add meat patties and cook for 5 minutes on each side. Remove meat to heated serving dish and keep warm.

Pour fat off skillet. Add sour cream and consommé and cook for 2 minutes. Correct seasoning. Bring to boil, stirring constantly and scraping bottom of skillet until brown crust is dissolved. Pour over meat. Serve hot.

Serves 4 to 6.

WINE: *A light red wine:*
        Red Bordeaux; Beaujolais; domestic claret.
        Or a chilled dry white wine:
        Pouilly-Fuissé; white Côtes du Rhône; Alsatian Riesling; Pinot Blanc.
        Or a rosé wine.

TOURNEDOS

"Tournedos" is deluxe steak. Like filet mignon, it is cut from the tenderest part of the filet. Tournedos is a round cut, about 2 inches in diameter and 1 inch thick. Needless to say, it is expensive.

It may be broiled, or sautéed in butter. It is generally preferred sautéed because the broiling makes it a little too dry. It is cooked rare or medium rare—never well-done. To sauté: cook tournedos in heated butter over brisk flame for 4 to 5 minutes each side. Salt and pepper to taste.

TOURNEDOS MORATEUR

8 tournedos, sautéed in butter   8 slices French bread,
3 anchovy filets, chopped   fried in butter
1 tablesp. butter   1 cup Madeira sauce*

Blend together anchovies and butter. Arrange slices of fried bread on heated serving dish. Remove sautéed tournedos from pan and place one tournedos on each slice of fried bread. Keep warm.

To pan in which tournedos have cooked, add Madeira

* Recipe given on page 129.

sauce and anchovy mixture. Heat, but do not allow to
boil. Pour over tournedos. Serve hot.

Serves 4.

Serve with matchstick potatoes.

WINE: A great Bordeaux or a great French Burgundy.

TOURNEDOS "INNKEEPER"

8 tournedos, sautéed in
  butter
8 slices French bread, fried
  in butter
¼ cup Madeira wine
1 teasp. finely chopped small
  white onions

¼ cup consommé
½ cup fresh or canned sliced
  mushrooms
½ teasp. salt
¼ teasp. freshly ground
  pepper
1 tablesp. manié butter*

Arrange slices of fried bread on heated serving dish
and keep warm. Remove sautéed tournedos from pan and
place one tournedos on each slice of fried bread.

To pan in which tournedos have cooked, add Madeira
wine and cook, scraping the bottom of the pan until the
brown crust is dissolved. Add onions and consommé.
Cook over brisk flame for 5 minutes. Add mushrooms,
salt, and pepper, and cook for 10 minutes. Add manié
butter and continue cooking, stirring constantly, for 3
minutes. Cover tournedos with mushroom mixture. Serve
hot.

Serves 4.

Serve with matchstick potatoes.

Optional: Budget permitting, garnish each tournedos
with slice of truffle.

WINE: *A great Bordeaux or a great French Burgundy.*

TOURNEDOS WITH CREAM

8 tournedos, sautéed in
  butter
8 thin slices French bread,
  warmed in oven
⅛ cup port wine
⅛ cup consommé

½ cup chopped fresh or
  canned mushrooms
½ teasp. salt
¼ teasp. freshly ground
  pepper
¼ cup sour cream

* Recipe given on page 125.

Arrange slices of warmed bread on heated serving dish. Remove sautéed tournedos from pan and place one tournedos on each slice of bread. Keep warm.

To pan in which tournedos have cooked, add wine and cook, scraping the bottom of pan until brown crust is dissolved. Add consommé and mushrooms. Cook for 10 minutes. Add cream and cook over low flame for 5 minutes, stirring constantly. Pour cream sauce over tournedos. Serve hot.

Serves 4.

Serve with French-fried potatoes.

Optional: Place a slice of foie gras on each tournedos before adding the mushroom mixture.

WINE: A great Bordeaux or a great French Burgundy.

VEAL CUTLETS FOYOT

Foyot was a famous Paris restaurant located just across the way from the Senate building. Senators and businessmen used to patronize it, and the splendid Foyot cuisine and cellar did much to iron out political enmity or conflicting interests. It was torn down to enlarge the street, and what remains of Foyot is only the souvenir of its contribution to great French cuisine.

Most of the specialties of the restaurant were superb, but much beyond the housewife's skill. "Cutlets Foyot," which was one of the restaurant's prides, is one of the very few that can be easily made at home.

2 lbs. loin of veal, cut into 4 equal slices	¼ cup finely chopped onions
½ teasp. salt	¼ cup fresh bread crumbs
¼ teasp. freshly ground pepper	¼ cup grated Swiss cheese
	½ cup dry white wine
1 tablesp. butter	3 tablesp. melted butter
	¼ cup consommé

Salt and pepper cutlets. Heat butter in small, heavy skillet. Add onions and cook until golden. In a bowl, combine bread crumbs and Swiss cheese.

Spread 1 tablespoon cooked onions on one side of each

cutlet. Cover with crumb-and-cheese mixture. Press cutlets with flat edge of a knife to make mixture stick.

Sprinkle remaining onions in an ovenproof dish. Place cutlets in dish side by side. Add wine and cover cutlets with melted butter. Bake uncovered for 2 hours, basting occasionally with liquid from pan. When liquid has evaporated, continue basting with consommé. Serve hot in baking dish.

Serves 4.

WINE: *A light red wine:*
        Red Bordeaux; Beaujolais; domestic claret.
        Or a chilled dry white wine:
        Bordeaux Graves; Pouilly-Fuissé; white Côtes du Rhône; Alsatian Riesling; Pinot Blanc.
        Or a rosé wine.

VEAL CUTLETS GUYENNE

2 lbs. loin of veal, cut into 4 equal slices	2 tablesp. chopped parsley
4 anchovy filets	1 tablesp. chopped scallion
2 small gherkin pickles	1 tablesp. finely chopped onion
4 strips bacon, cut in two	1 clove garlic, crushed
1/3 cup dry white Bordeaux wine	pinch of pepper
1/3 cup consommé	2 egg yolks
	salt to taste

With sharp knife, make small incisions in cutlets. Cut anchovy filets and gherkins into small pieces. Fill incisions in cutlets with pieces of anchovy and gherkin.

Line bottom of heavy skillet with bacon strips. Arrange cutlets on top of bacon. Add wine, consommé, parsley, scallion, onion, garlic, and pepper. Bring to boil. Cover and cook over low flame for 1½ hours, or until meat is very tender. Remove cutlets to heated serving dish and keep warm. Raise heat under skillet and continue cooking for 5 minutes more. Blend with egg yolks. Correct seasoning. Cook for a few seconds, until sauce thickens. Pour sauce over cutlets. Serve hot.

Serves 4.

WINE: *A chilled dry white wine:*
Bordeaux Graves; French chablis; Pouilly-Fuissé;
white Côtes du Rhône.

VEAL CUTLETS NIÇOISE

1 lb. veal cutlets, pounded thin	3 tablesp. olive oil
½ cup flour	1 clove garlic, finely chopped
½ teasp. salt	1 4-oz. can sliced mushrooms, drained
¼ teasp. pepper	¼ cup port wine

Combine flour, salt, and pepper. Dredge cutlets with
flour mixture. In large, heavy skillet, heat oil. Add cutlets and garlic. Cook over brisk flame for 10 minutes
on each side, or until well browned. Remove meat to
heated serving dish and keep warm. Add mushrooms to
pan, and cook for 5 minutes. Remove mushrooms to
serving dish and keep warm. Raise heat. Add port wine
and heat, stirring until brown parts which stick to the
bottom of pan are dissolved. Do not allow to boil. Pour
over meat. Serve hot.

Serves 4.

WINE: *A full-bodied red wine:*
French red Bordeaux; French red Burgundy; red
Côtes du Rhône; domestic claret or Burgundy;
Pinot Noir; Cabernet.

COTES de VEAU BONNE FEMME
(Veal Chops)

4 veal chops, 1-inch thick	¼ teasp. pepper
¼ cup flour	4 tablesp. butter
½ teasp. salt	16 small white onions
3 potatoes, peeled and diced	

Dredge chops with flour. Salt and pepper. In large,
heavy saucepan, heat 2 tablespoons butter. Add chops,
and cook until chops are well browned on both sides.

Meanwhile, in another saucepan, heat remaining butter. Add onions and cook for 10 minutes, or until onions are slightly browned.

To pan in which chops are cooking, add browned onions and potatoes. Cover and simmer gently for 1 hour, or until chops are fork-tender. Serve hot.

Serves 4.

WINE: *A light red wine:*
Red Bordeaux; Beaujolais; domestic claret.
Or a chilled dry white wine:
Bordeaux Graves; Pouilly-Fuissé; white Côtes du Rhône; Alsatian Riesling; Pinot Blanc.
Or a rosé wine.

PAUPIETTES de VEAU
(Rolled Veal)

8 slices leg of veal, pounded thin	4 strips bacon, cut into 2 pieces
2 tablesp. chopped parsley	2 tablesp. butter
2 tablesp. finely chopped scallions	1 tablesp. chopped onions
	2 tablesp. chopped celery
½ teasp. salt	3 sprigs parsley
¼ teasp. pepper	¼ cup consommé

Combine parsley, scallion, salt, and pepper. Sprinkle each slice of meat with parsley mixture. Lay a piece of bacon over mixture. Roll slice of meat and tie with a string. Heat butter in large, heavy skillet. Add onions, celery, and parsley. Cook over low flame for 5 minutes. Arrange rolled meat on bottom of pan. Cook uncovered for 10 minutes, turning two or three times so that meat rolls are whitened on all sides. Do not allow meat to brown. Cover. Simmer for 1 hour, turning twice during the last half-hour of cooking. Discard strings. Remove meat to heated serving dish and keep warm.

Add consommé to pan. Bring to boil and cook for 5 minutes. Pour over meat. Serve hot.

Serves 4.

Serve with rice.

WINE: *A light red wine:*
Red Bordeaux; Beaujolais; domestic claret.

Or a chilled dry white wine:
Bordeaux Graves; Pouilly-Fuissé; white Côtes du
Rhône; Alsatian Riesling; Pinot Blanc.
Or a rosé wine.

BLANQUETTE de VEAU
(Blanket of Veal)

This is one of the perfect dishes of "cuisine bourgeoise." It is economical, nourishing, delicate, and tasty.
In fact, it is so excellent that "grande cuisine" has
adopted it.

With new "lettres de noblesse," blanquette de veau has
exchanged its plebian name for a more aristocratic one,
so call it "Blanquette de Veau à l'Ancienne" if you wish,
but don't change anything in the recipe: it is the same.
Blanket by any other name . . .

2 lbs. breast or shoulder
    of veal
4 cups water
12 small white onions
1 medium-size carrot, cut
    into pieces approximately
    ½ inch long
1 medium-size onion studded
    with 2 cloves
1 bay leaf
pinch of thyme

½ teasp. salt
¼ teasp. white pepper
1 tablesp. butter
1 tablesp. flour
½ cup fresh or canned
    mushrooms, sliced
⅛ cup heavy cream
2 egg yolks
1 teasp. lemon juice
1 tablesp. chopped parsley

Cut meat into 12 pieces. Place veal in large, heavy
saucepan. Add water. Bring to boil. Skim. Add white onions, carrot, onion studded with cloves, bay leaf, thyme,
salt, and pepper. Cover and simmer for 1½ hours, or
until meat is tender. Remove meat, small white onions,
and carrot to heated serving dish and keep warm. Discard bay leaf and onion studded with cloves.

In another saucepan melt butter. Stir in flour and cook
until smooth. Add cooking liquid and mushrooms, and
cook over low flame for 15 minutes, stirring occasionally.
In a bowl, combine cream and yolks. Stir in 5 table-

spoons of sauce from pan, one at a time. Then stir egg
mixture into sauce in pan. Add lemon juice. Cook over
low flame for 5 minutes without allowing to boil, stirring
constantly. Pour sauce over meat. Sprinkle with parsley.
Serve hot.

Serves 4 to 6.

Blanquette de veau is traditionally served with rice,
but noodles or boiled potatoes are also very good with it.

WINE: *A chilled dry white wine:*
　　　　Bordeaux Graves; Alsatian Riesling; Pouilly-
　　　　Fuissé; French chablis; Pinot Blanc.

ROAST VEAL WITH HERBS

2½ lbs. boneless veal roast	3 tablesp. salad oil
1 teasp. chopped parsley	½ teasp. salt
2 teasp. chopped scallion	¼ teasp. pepper
2 teasp. chopped onion	pinch of grated nutmeg
½ teasp. thyme	1 tablesp. vinegar
1 crushed bay leaf	1 tablesp. butter
4 chopped mushrooms	1 tablesp. flour
(not peeled)	

In deep bowl, combine parsley, scallion, onion, thyme,
bay leaf, mushrooms, oil, salt, pepper, and nutmeg. Add
veal. Let stand for 3 hours, turning occasionally. Place
veal on aluminum foil. Pour herb mixture over meat and
wrap foil carefully. Cook in oven at 350° F. for 1½ hours,
or until meat is tender. Unwrap. Scrape off herbs and
reserve for further use. Cut meat into thin slices. Place
slices on heated serving dish and keep warm.

In small saucepan, combine herbs, juice from roast,
and vinegar. Work butter and flour to a smooth paste
and add to the pan. Cook for 5 minutes. Serve sauce in
sauce boat.

Serves 4 to 6.

WINE: *A light red wine:*
　　　　Red Bordeaux; Beaujolais; domestic claret.
　　　　Or a chilled dry white wine:

Pouilly-Fuissé; white Côtes du Rhône; Alsatian
Riesling; Pinot Blanc.
Or a rosé wine.

VEAL WITH CARROTS

3 lbs. leg (or loin) veal roast	2 cups water
2 tablesp. butter	½ teasp. salt
12 small white onions	¼ teasp. freshly ground pepper
12 medium-size carrots, sliced	

In Dutch oven or large, heavy saucepan, heat butter.
Add meat and cook until well browned on all sides. Add
onions and carrots. Cover tightly and cook over very low
flame for 20 minutes. Add water, salt, and pepper. Bring
to boil. Cover and simmer gently for 1½ hours, or until
meat is very tender. Cut meat into thin slices. Arrange
slices in center of heated serving dish. Surround meat
with onions and carrots. Pour sauce over meat. Serve hot.
   Serves 6.

WINE: *A light red wine:*
         Red Bordeaux; Beaujolais; domestic claret.
         Or a chilled dry white wine:
         Bordeaux Graves; Pouilly-Fuissé; white Côtes du
         Rhône; Alsatian Riesling; Pinot Blanc.
         Or a rosé wine.

LAMB "PERSILLE"

1 leg of lamb, approximately 5 lbs.	⅛ cup finely chopped scallion (white part only)
½ teasp. salt	1 small clove garlic, finely chopped
¼ teasp. pepper	
4 thin slices salt pork	⅛ cup finely chopped parsley
½ cup fresh bread crumbs	⅓ cup dry white wine
⅓ cup consommé	

Salt and pepper meat. Wrap meat in salt pork slices.
Place in baking dish and bake at 400° F. for 45 minutes,

turning once. In a bowl, combine bread crumbs, scallion, garlic, and parsley. Mix well. Add mixture to pan and continue baking for 10 minutes, or until bread mixture is golden. Remove meat from pan and cut into thin slices. Arrange slices on heated serving dish and keep warm.

Meanwhile, add wine and consommé to pan. Bring to boil over brisk flame. Reduce flame and simmer for 5 minutes. Cover slices of meat mixture from pan. Serve hot with sauté potatoes.

Serves 6.

WINE: A red Bordeaux.

NAVARIN DE MOUTON
(Lamb Stew)

2 lbs. shoulder of lamb, cut for stew	1 medium-size onion, studded with a clove
2 tablesp. butter	1 bay leaf
¼ teasp. granulated sugar	pinch of thyme
1 tablesp. flour	½ teasp. salt
2 cups lukewarm water	¼ teasp. pepper
1 cup consommé	12 medium-size potatoes, peeled and quartered

In Dutch oven or large, heavy saucepan, heat butter. Add meat and cook until browned on all sides. Add sugar and cook for 3 minutes, stirring constantly. Pour fat off pan. Sprinkle meat with flour, and cook until brown, stirring constantly. Stir in water and consommé. Add onion, bay leaf, thyme, salt, and pepper. Bring to boil. Cover and simmer for 1 hour. Add potatoes. Cover and continue simmering for another hour. Serve hot.

Serves 4 to 6.

WINE: *A full-bodied red wine:*
        French red Bordeaux; French red Burgundy; red Côtes du Rhône; domestic claret or Burgundy; Pinot Noir; Cabernet.

SHOULDER OF LAMB "BOULANGERE"

1 lamb shoulder, boned and rolled	8 medium-size potatoes, peeled and sliced
2 tablesp. lard	1 medium-size onion, thinly sliced
½ teasp. salt	2 tablesp. butter
¼ teasp. pepper	1 tablesp. chopped parsley
1 cup water	

Grease large baking dish with 1 tablespoon lard. In large, heavy skillet or saucepan, heat remaining lard. Add meat and cook for 10 minutes, or until meat is browned on all sides. Season with salt and pepper. Remove meat to baking dish. Add water to pan and bring to boil.

Meanwhile, surround meat with potatoes and onions. Pour liquid from pan over potatoes and onions, and dot with butter. Bake at 400° F. for 1 hour, basting occasionally.

For serving: Cut meat into thin slices and arrange slices in center of baking dish. Sprinkle with parsley. Serve hot. Serves 4.

WINE: A red Bordeaux.

HARICOT DE MOUTON
(Lamb with Beans)

2 lbs. shoulder of lamb, cut for stew	2 tablesp. tomato paste
2 cups dried beans	½ teasp. salt
2 tablesp. salad oil	¼ teasp. pepper
1 tablesp. flour	1 small bay leaf
1 clove garlic, crushed	pinch of thyme
2 cups water	2 sprigs parsley
	2 tablesp. chopped parsley

Soak beans overnight. Cook in salted water for 45 minutes. Drain and set aside.

Meanwhile, in Dutch oven or large, heavy saucepan, heat oil. Add meat and cook until browned on all sides. Pour fat off pan. Add flour and cook until well browned, stirring constantly. Add garlic and cook for 2 minutes. Add water, tomato paste, salt, pepper, bay leaf, thyme, and sprigs of parsley. Bring to boil. Cover and

simmer for 45 minutes. Add beans. Bring to boil. Cover
and simmer gently for 1 hour. Discard bay leaf and
sprigs of parsley. Sprinkle with chopped parsley.

Serve in deep serving dish or in individual casseroles.
Serve hot.

Serves 4 to 6.

WINE: *A full-bodied red wine:*
French red Bordeaux; French red Burgundy; red
Côtes du Rhône; domestic claret or Burgundy;
Pinot Noir; Cabernet.

CASSOULET TOULOUSAIN
(Dried Beans and Meat)

Each region of France has its own Cassoulet which is
somewhat different from the others. But Cassoulet Toul-
ousain (from the city of Toulouse in the French Pyre-
nees) has achieved a well-deserved fame, and is served all
over France.

When possible, Cassoulet includes "oie confite" (goose
preserved in its own fat) . Duck may replace goose. When
neither goose nor duck is available, Cassoulet is still
superb.

If you wish to serve an hors-d'oeuvre, serve a very light
one (clams, oysters, etc.) . Cassoulet with a tossed green
salad and the lightest desert makes a plentiful meal.
With it, you will drink a full-bodied red wine.

Cassoulet can be prepared in advance and reheated in
the oven.

3 cups white dried beans,
  soaked overnight
1 tablesp. salt
¼ teasp. thyme
1 bay leaf
½ lb. garlic sausage or
  Polish sausage
½ lb. lean salt pork, diced
4 tablesp. chicken fat or lard

2 lbs. shoulder or breast of
  lamb, cut for stew
2 large onions, chopped
¼ cup tomato paste (4
  tablesp.)
2 cloves garlic, crushed
¼ teasp. pepper
3 tablesp. fresh bread
  crumbs

Drain beans and place in kettle or large saucepan.

Cover with water. Add ½ teaspoon salt, thyme, bay leaf, and sausage. Bring to boil, and simmer slowly for 30 minutes. Remove sausage and set aside. Continue simmering for 1 hour.

Meanwhile, in a small saucepan, cook salt pork in boiling water for 5 minutes. Drain and set aside. In large saucepan, heat chicken fat. Add lamb. Add remaining salt and cook until slightly browned on all sides. Pour off excess fat. Add onions and cook until onions are well browned. Cover with water. Add tomato paste, garlic, pepper, and boiled salt pork. Correct seasoning. Bring to boil, and simmer gently.

Drain beans and add to pan. Return sausage to pan. Cover and simmer for 1 hour, or until meat and beans are tender. Rub the inside of a very large ovenproof dish with a clove of garlic. Remove lamb and sausage from pan and turn the contents of pan into ovenproof dish. Cut sausage into slices approximately ½ inch thick. Arrange lamb and sausage on top of beans. Sprinkle with bread crumbs. Dot with butter. Broil under broiling flame for 5 minutes, or until well browned. Serve hot.

Serves 4 to 6.

WINE: *A chilled dry white wine:*
        Bordeaux Graves; Alsatian Riesling; Pouilly-Fuissé; French chablis; Pinot Blanc.

MUTTON CHOPS ARLESIENNE

4 mutton chops	pinch of thyme
2 tablesp. butter	pinch of marjoram
¼ cup dry white wine	1 clove garlic, crushed
1½ cups canned tomatoes	1 tablesp. minced parsley

salt, pepper

In skillet, cook mutton chops in heated butter till well done. Salt and pepper. Remove chops to heated platter and keep warm. Pour excess fat from skillet. Add wine to skillet, and scrape bottom until brown crust is dissolved. Cook over high flame for 3 minutes, or until wine is nearly cooked away. Add tomatoes, thyme, marjoram, and garlic, with salt and pepper to taste. Cook over high flame for 10 minutes. Return chops to skillet. Sprinkle with parsley. Serve hot in skillet.

Serves 4.

Serve with rice.

WINE: *A light red wine:*
Red Bordeaux; Beaujolais; domestic claret.

PORK CHOPS PIQUANTE

1 teasp. butter	1 medium-size onion,
4 pork chops	chopped
½ teasp. salt	3 tablesp. wine vinegar
¼ teasp. pepper	¼ cup sauce piquante*

In heavy skillet, heat butter. Add chops and cook, turning once, for 20 minutes, or until chops are browned and thoroughly cooked through. Remove chops to heated serving dish and keep warm. Pour fat off skillet, leaving about 1 teaspoon of fat. Add onions to skillet and cook, stirring constantly, for 2 minutes, or until onions are golden. Add vinegar and continue cooking for 2 minutes more, or until liquid is reduced to approximately 1 tablespoon. Add sauce piquante. Bring to boil, stirring constantly, and then simmer for 2 minutes. Pour sauce over chops. Serve hot.

Serves 4.

WINE: *A chilled dry white wine:*
Bordeaux Graves; French chablis; Pouilly-Fuissé; white Côtes du Rhône.

CALF'S LIVER SAUTE

1 lb. calf's liver, cut into slices ¼-inch thick	¼ cup flour
	2 tablesp. butter
½ teasp. salt	⅛ cup tarragon vinegar
¼ teasp. pepper	2 tablesp. chopped parsley
1 lemon cut into thin slices	

* Recipe given on page 130.

Salt and pepper liver. Dredge with flour. In large skillet, heat butter. Add liver, and cook one side for 5 minutes. Turn, and cook other side for 4 minutes. Remove liver to heated serving dish and keep warm. Add vinegar to skillet and cook over brisk flame, scraping the bottom of skillet until the brown crust is dissolved. Pour over liver. Sprinkle liver with parsley and garnish with slices of lemon.

Serves 4.

Serve with boiled potatoes.

WINE: *A light red wine:*
         Red Bordeaux; Beaujolais; domestic claret.
         Or a chilled dry white wine:
         Pouilly-Fuissé; white Côtes du Rhône; Alsatian Riesling; Pinot Blanc.
         Or a rosé wine.

CALF'S LIVER WITH GRAPES

1 lb. calf's liver, cut into slices ¼-in. thick	¼ cup butter
½ teasp. salt	¼ cup sweet white Bordeaux wine
¼ teasp. pepper	2 tablesp. chicken broth
¼ cup flour	2 lbs. seedless green grapes

Salt and pepper liver. Dredge with flour. In large, heavy skillet, heat 2 tablespoons butter. Add liver, and cook for 2 minutes each side. Remove liver to heated dish and keep warm. Pour fat off skillet. Add wine and chicken broth to skillet and cook over brisk flame, scraping the bottom of the skillet until the brown crust is dissolved. Bring to boil. Return liver to skillet. Cover. Simmer gently for 5 minutes.

Meanwhile stem and wash grapes. In small skillet, heat remaining butter. Add grapes to skillet and cook for 5 minutes, or until grapes are golden brown. Remove grapes and arrange in center of heated serving dish. Surround grapes with slices of liver. Pour sauce from liver skillet over slices.

Serves 4.

WINE: *A chilled white wine:*
DRY: Bordeaux Graves; Alsatian Riesling or Traminer; Sauvignon Blanc.
SWEET: Bordeaux Sauternes; Gewurztraminer; sweet Semillon.

VEAL KIDNEY WITH PORT WINE

4 veal kidneys	¼ teasp. freshly ground
¼ cup flour	pepper
2 tablesp. butter	pinch of grated nutmeg
2 tablesp. port wine	1 tablesp. chopped parsley
½ teasp. salt	6 slices French bread, fried in butter

Remove outer skin from kidneys and cut them into slices ½ inch thick. Dredge with flour. In large, heavy skillet, heat butter. Add kidneys and cook over brisk flame, turning them often, for 10 minutes, or until browned on all sides (do not overcook). Remove meat to heated serving dish and keep warm. To pan, add port wine, salt, pepper, and nutmeg, and heat, stirring until the brown parts which stick to the bottom of pan are dissolved. Do not allow to boil. Pour over meat. Sprinkle with parsley. Garnish with fried bread. Serve hot.
Serves 4.
WINE: *A light red wine:*
Red Bordeaux; Beaujolais; domestic claret.
Or a chilled dry white wine:
Bordeaux Graves; Pouilly-Fuissé; white Côtes du Rhône; Alsatian Riesling; Pinot Blanc.
Or a rosé wine.

CALVES' BRAINS
Preparation of Brains

2 calves' brains	1 bay leaf
1 teasp. salt	pinch of thyme
1 onion studded with 1 clove	4 peppercorns

Soak brains in cold water for 2 hours. Remove thin outer skin. Soak again in cold water for 3 hours.

Place brains in large saucepan. Cover with cold water. Add salt, onion, bay leaf, thyme, and peppercorns. Bring to boil. Cover and simmer for 20 minutes. Keep brains in cooking liquid until ready to use in recipe. Then remove brains and drain them.

CALVES' BRAINS BEURRE NOIR

2 cooked calves' brains	¼ teasp. pepper
½ teasp. salt	⅛ cup butter
	2 tablesp. vinegar

Arrange brains on heated serving dish. Keep warm.

In small skillet, melt butter and cook until butter is dark brown. Pour over brains. To skillet, add vinegar and cook briskly for 2 minutes. Pour over brains. Serve hot.

Serves 4.

Serve with boiled potatoes sprinkled with chopped parsley.

WINE: *A chilled dry white wine:*
Bordeaux Graves; Alsatian Riesling; Pouilly-Fuissé; French chablis; Pinot Blanc.

CALVES' BRAINS SAUTES

2 cooked calves' brains	¼ cup butter
⅛ cup flour	6 thin slices lemon
	1 tablesp. chopped parsley

Scallop brains. Dredge with flour. In large skillet, heat ⅛ cup butter. Add brains and cook for 10 minutes, or until well browned on all sides. Remove brains to heated serving dish and keep warm.

Meanwhile, in small skillet, heat remaining butter and cook for 5 minutes, or until butter is hazel brown. Pour over brains. Garnish with slices of lemon and sprinkle with parsley. Serve hot.

Serves 4.

Serve with boiled potatoes.

WINE: *A chilled dry white wine:*
        Bordeaux Graves; Alsatian Riesling; Pouilly-
        Fuissé; French chablis; Pinot Blanc.

BRAISED SWEETBREADS

2 pairs sweetbreads	1 teasp. salt
2 tablesp. butter	¼ teasp. freshly ground
1 medium-size carrot, sliced	pepper
2 tablesp. chopped onions	1 small bay leaf
1 strip bacon, cut into	½ cup consommé
small pieces	½ cup water
2 sprigs parsley	

Soak sweetbreads in cold water for 1 hour. Drain. Place
sweetbreads in heavy saucepan. Cover with fresh water.
Bring slowly to boil, and simmer gently for 5 minutes. Remove sweetbreads to bowl of ice water and let stand in
bowl for 5 minutes. Drain and dry on cloth. Remove the
part which is not edible, but do not remove the thin skin
on sweetbreads. Place sweetbreads in shallow dish and
cover with a plate pressing directly on them in order to
break the fibers, thus preventing them from contracting
when cooking.

In an ovenproof dish, melt butter. Add carrots, onions,
bacon, parsley, salt, pepper, and bay leaf. Bake at 450° F.
for 10 minutes. Add sweetbreads, consommé, and water
and continue baking, basting occasionally, for 45 minutes
more, or until meat is well browned on top. Remove meat
to heated serving dish. Pour sauce over meat.

Serves 4.

Serve with peas.

WINE: *A light red wine:*
        Red Bordeaux; Beaujolais; domestic claret.
        Or a chilled dry white wine:
        Pouilly-Fuissé; white Côtes du Rhône; Alsatian
        Riesling; Pinot Blanc.
        Or a rosé wine.

OX TONGUE, BOILED

1 fresh tongue	1 bay leaf
1 quart water	pinch of thyme
1 tablesp. wine vinegar	½ teasp. salt
2 medium-size onions, studded with one clove each	4 peppercorns

In a deep bowl, combine water and vinegar. Add tongue, and soak for 2 hours.

In Dutch oven or large kettle, place tongue. Cover with fresh water. Add onions, bay leaf, thyme, salt, and peppercorns. Bring to boil. Cover and simmer for 3 hours, or until meat is tender. Remove tongue and skin it.

OX TONGUE, BRAISED

1 boiled ox tongue	2 carrots, sliced
2 strips of bacon, cut into pieces 1 inch long	2 medium-size onions, sliced
	⅓ cup dry white wine
2 cups consommé	

In Dutch oven or large, heavy saucepan, place bacon, carrots, and onions. Cook over low flame for 5 minutes. Add wine and ½ cup consommé. Bring to boil, and simmer for 20 minutes, or until liquid is reduced to 2 tablespoons. Add tongue and remaining consommé. Bring to boil. Cover and simmer for 30 minutes. Remove tongue and cut into thin slices. Serve sauce in sauceboat. Serve hot.

Serve with noodles.

WINE: *A light red wine:*
Red Bordeaux; Beaujolais; domestic claret.
Or a chilled dry white wine:
Bordeaux Graves; Pouilly-Fuissé; white Côtes du Rhône; Alsatian Riesling; Pinot Blanc.
Or a rosé wine.

OX TONGUE SAUCE PIQUANTE

8 slices boiled tongue   1 cup sauce piquante*

In large, heavy saucepan, heat sauce piquante. Add slices of tongue and simmer gently for 10 minutes. Serve hot.

Serves 4.

Serve with boiled potatoes.

WINE: *A chilled dry white wine:*
          Bordeaux Graves; Alsatian Riesling; Pouilly-Fuissé; French chablis; Pinot Blanc.

TRIPE

By far the most famous tripe dish is "tripes à la mode de Caen," but the best Americans can do about it is to put it on the list of dishes they intend to try if and when they go to France.

The preparation of tripes à la mode de Caen is a little more than the average French cook is ready to undertake —so it is doubtful that the American housewife would take the trouble to do it. Even so, the best American recipe for tripes à la mode de Caen would only be a second-rate adaptation of the real one because some of the necessary varieties of tripe are not available in this country.

However, there are many other delectable recipes which do not require special knowledge or ingredients. Both "tripe Lyonnaise" and "tripe Poulette" are delicious family dishes.

TRIPE LYONNAISE

1 lb. tripe   3 medium-size onions, sliced
½ teasp. salt   1 tablesp. vinegar
¼ teasp. pepper   1 tablesp. chopped parsley
2 tablesp. butter

Wash tripe, and place in Dutch oven or large, heavy saucepan. Cover with water. Add salt and pepper. Bring

* Recipe given on page 130.

to boil. Cover and simmer for 4 hours, or until meat is tender. Drain. Cut tripe into small pieces.

In large skillet, heat 1 tablespoon butter. Add tripe and cook, stirring occasionally, for 20 minutes, or until tripe is well browned. Meanwhile, in another skillet, melt remaining butter. Add onions and cook, stirring occasionally, until onions are browned. In heated serving dish, combine tripe and onions. Add vinegar to pan in which tripe has cooked, and cook for 3 minutes. Pour over tripe. Sprinkle with parsley. Serve hot.

Serves 4.

WINE: *A red wine:*
Red Bordeaux; French red Burgundy; red Côtes du Rhône; domestic claret or Burgundy.

TRIPE POULETTE

1 lb. tripe	2 cups clear chicken broth
1 teasp. salt	2 sprigs parsley
¼ teasp. pepper	2 egg yolks
2 tablesp. butter	juice of one lemon
1 tablesp. flour	1 tablesp. finely chopped parsley

Wash tripe, and place in Dutch oven or large, heavy saucepan. Cover with water. Add ½ teaspoon salt, and pepper. Bring to boil. Cover and simmer for 4 hours, or until tripe is tender. Drain. Cut into small pieces. Set aside.

In large, heavy saucepan, heat 1 tablespoon butter. Add flour and cook for 1 minute, stirring constantly. Stir in chicken broth. Add remaining salt and sprigs of parsley. Bring to boil, stirring occasionally. Add tripe. Lower flame, and simmer for 30 minutes. Discard sprigs of parsley. Blend with egg yolks. Off fire, add lemon juice, chopped parsley, and remaining butter cut into small pieces. Stir until butter is melted. Serve hot.

Serves 4.

Serve with boiled potatoes.

WINE: *Apple cider.*
       Or a chilled dry white wine:
       Bordeaux Graves; French chablis; Alsatian Riesling; white Côtes du Rhône.

SAUCISSE PAYSANNE
(Country-Style Sausage)

4 medium-size carrots	pinch of thyme
2 small white turnips	1 bay leaf
4 small white onions, coarsely chopped	2 tablesp. chopped parsley
	½ teasp. salt
3 stalks celery	¼ teasp. pepper
4 leeks (white part only)	¼ cup consommé
1 1-lb.-12-oz. can tomatoes	1½ lbs. Polish sausage

Clean and cut vegetables into pieces 1-inch long. In a large, heavy saucepan combine carrots, turnips, onions, celery, leeks, tomatoes, thyme, bay leaf, parsley, salt, and pepper. Add consommé. Bring to boil and cook for 5 minutes. Add sausage. Cover and simmer for 1 hour. To serve, arrange vegetables in center of serving dish. Cut sausages into slices ½-inch thick and arrange slices in a crown around vegetables. Serve hot.

WINE: *A light red wine:*
       Red Bordeaux; Beaujolais; domestic claret.
       Or a chilled dry white wine:
       Pouilly-Fuissé; white Côtes du Rhône; Alsatian Riesling; Pinot Blanc.
       Or a rosé wine.

SAUSAGE IN WINE

1½ lbs. pork sausage	1 tablesp. flour
¼ cup water	1 cup consommé
¾ cup dry white wine	1 egg yolk
1 tablesp. butter	1 tablesp. lemon juice

Place sausage in large skillet. Add water. Cover and simmer for 5 minutes. Drain off water and continue cooking for 10 minutes more, or until sausage is well browned. Pour fat off skillet. Add wine and cook until wine is reduced to half the original volume.

Meanwhile, heat butter in small, heavy saucepan. Add flour. Stir in consommé and cook over low flame for 10 minutes.

Remove sausage to heated serving dish and keep warm. To consommé mixture, add reduced wine from sausage skillet. Blend with yolk. Add lemon juice. Correct seasoning. Cook for a few seconds, until sauce thickens. Pour over sausage. Serve hot.

Serves 4.

WINE: *A light red wine:*
        Red Bordeaux; Beaujolais; domestic claret.
        Or a chilled dry white wine:
        Pouilly-Fuissé; white Côtes du Rhône; Alsatian Riesling; Pinot Blanc.
        Or a rosé wine.

CIVET de LAPIN
(Rabbit Stew)

1 2½-3-lb. ready-to-cook rabbit	1 small clove garlic, crushed
¼ lb. salt pork, diced	1 teasp. salt
4 tablesp. butter	¼ teasp. pepper
2 tablesp. chopped onion	1 cup dry white wine
	1 tablesp. chopped parsley

Cut rabbit into serving pieces. Reserve liver.

In small saucepan, cook salt pork in boiling water for 5 minutes. Drain.

In Dutch oven or heavy saucepan, heat 2 tablespoons butter. Add salt pork and cook for 5 minutes, or until slightly brown. Remove and set aside. Add rabbit to pan, and cook for 10 minutes, or until rabbit is slightly browned on all sides. Add onion and garlic and continue cooking for 5 minutes, stirring occasionally. Return salt pork to pan. Add salt, pepper, and wine. Bring to boil. Cover and continue cooking briskly for 20 minutes.

Meanwhile, chop liver and rub through a fine sieve.

Remove rabbit to heated serving dish and keep warm.
Add liver purée to pan, and cook for a few seconds
until sauce thickens, stirring constantly. Off fire, add remaining butter cut into small pieces, stirring until butter
is melted. Pour over rabbit. Sprinkle with parsley. Serve
hot.

Serves 4 to 6.

Serve with boiled potatoes.

WINE: *A red wine:*

Red Bordeaux; French red Burgundy; red Côtes
du Rhône; domestic claret or Burgundy.

CHOUCROUTE GARNIE
("Garnished" Sauerkraut)

4 lbs. sauerkraut	2 bay leaves
1 tablesp. butter	1/4 teasp. thyme
3/4 lb. bacon, diced	salt to taste
1 large onion, studded with 3 cloves	2 cups dry white Alsatian wine
1 lb. Polish-style sausage, cut into 2-inch pieces	3 cups water
1 lb. smoked pork shoulder	12 medium-size potatoes, peeled and boiled
1 carrot, sliced	12 frankfurters

10 juniper berries ⎫ tied in a
6 peppercorns ⎭ cheesecloth bag

Place sauerkraut in deep bowl. Pull it to pieces, sepa-
rating the leaves. Fill bowl with water. Let stand 15
minutes. Drain. Wash sauerkraut under running water.
Drain again, and press in both hands until all water is
squeezed out. Meanwhile, melt butter in Dutch oven or
large, heavy pan. Add bacon and onion. Cook until
browned. Add sausage and pork shoulder. Cook until
meat is browned. Remove meat and set aside. Add sauerkraut to pan and cook, stirring constantly, until sauerkraut is slightly browned. Add carrot, bag of juniper
berries and peppercorns, bay leaves, thyme, salt, wine, and
water. Bring to boil. Cover and simmer over low flame
for 3 hours. Return meat to pan. Cover and continue

simmering for 45 minutes. Add potatoes and frankfurters. Cover and continue simmering for 15 minutes
more.

For serving: On center of large heated platter, arrange
sauerkraut in a dome. Cut pork into thin slices and
arrange on sauerkraut. Decorate with frankfurters. Surround with pieces of sausage alternated with potatoes.
Serve hot.

Serves 6 to 8.

Drink: *beer.*

CHOU FARCI
(Stuffed Cabbage)

1 cabbage	3 slices salt pork
1½ teasp. salt	1 carrot, sliced
1 cup leftover meat, ground	1 medium-size onion, sliced
½ lb. sausage meat	2 cups consommé
¼ teasp. pepper	1 teasp. arrowroot,
1 tablesp. chopped parsley	dissolved in water

Wash and trim cabbage. Remove as much as possible
of the hard core. Place cabbage in large saucepan and
cover with cold water. Add 1 teaspoon salt. Bring slowly
to boil. Let boil for 2 minutes. Drain in a colander in
order to keep the cabbage intact.

In mixing bowl, combine leftover meat, sausage meat,
remaining salt, pepper, and parsley. Mix well.

Place cabbage in a bowl, leaves up. Carefully remove
core, leaving bottom of cabbage. Stuff cavity with part
of meat mixture. Carefully open leaves and stuff between
leaves with meat mixture. Wrap stuffed cabbage in slices
of salt pork. Tie with a string.

In heavy saucepan, large enough to hold whole cabbage, place carrot and onion. Add cabbage. Add consommé. Bring to boil. Cover and simmer gently for 3
hours.

For serving: Remove cabbage from pan and drain.
Place on heated serving dish and keep warm.

Bring to boil cooking liquid and continue boiling for

15 minutes, or until liquid is reduced to 1 cup. Add
arrowroot dissolved in water, and continue boiling for
a few seconds, until liquid thickens. Pour over cabbage.
Serve hot.

Serves 6 to 8.

WINE: *A full-bodied red wine:*
French red Bordeaux; French red Burgundy; red
Côtes du Rhône; domestic claret or Burgundy;
Pinot Noir; Cabernet.

Chapter VIII

Sauces

ONE OF THE MERITS of French cooking is its diversity. There is no one dominant taste which typifies French cuisine. Other countries have one or more recurrent combinations, and you could guess blindfolded the origin of the dish. Not so with French dishes: some are light and delicate; some are very tasty; some are pungent; some have a sturdy flavor of cooking with oil, tomatoes, and garlic; some, the subtle harmony of butter, cream, and eggs.

What gives to fish or meat so many aspects and flavors are principally the sauces in which they are cooked or which accompany them.

Sauces are of the utmost importance to the French housewife because they allow her to make fine dishes with less expensive cuts. Although there are innumerable recipes for tournedos (steaks) with elaborate sauces, prime cuts which can be grilled, broiled, or roasted do not really require more than grilling, broiling, or roasting. Less tender cuts have to be cooked for a long time and lose much of their savor in the process if they are not enhanced by the right sauce.

Fish when absolutely fresh, just out of the water, does not need any accompaniment. Simply grilled or broiled with salt and pepper, and dotted with butter (and of course a few drops of lemon) , it is a regal dish, but we all know from experience how flavorless fish can be when it reaches the market in a city far from the shore.

Sauce brings out the faint flavor of fish and the reduced flavor of meat, and adds a wonderful background to these flavors. Sauce brings out the taste of the principal ingredients; it does not cover or alter it. To mask the taste of meat with the sauce is a culinary heresy.

The role of the sauce is also to compensate for the dryness of the dish, and in France when you have sauce you have plenty of it, and the vegetables are carefully selected so that they also are good with sauce when mixed on the plate.

The French are very severe with sauces. They will condemn a dish with the sharp comment that "the sauce has the taste of flour," which is a death sentence. Although basically there is flour in practically all hot sauces, it is held to a minimum and cooked in such a way that the floury taste never comes out.

Most of the time this is achieved by making a "roux." This means that the butter and flour are cooked and then a tasty liquid (practically never plain water) is added. This mixture simmers until well blended and the taste of the flour disappears entirely.

When a sauce has to be thickened at the last minute, the French use egg yolks or "beurre manié." Egg yolks make a velvety sauce of extreme fineness. Beurre manié is so easy to prepare and finishes a sauce so quickly and so beautifully that it is surprising to see it mentioned in "grande cuisine" recipes only.

Cold sauces are used in much the same way as mayonnaise or Worcestershire, but their variety offers the full gamut of matching or contrasting flavors.

How to Blend with Egg Yolks

One egg yolk is generally sufficient to blend a sauce.
Two makes the sauce richer and more velvety.

To use yolk in a sauce, first place yolk in a bowl. Break
it with a spoon, stirring 1 spoonful of the hot liquid to
blend. When well mixed, stir in another spoonful. Alto-
gether, stir in a total of 4 or 5 spoonfuls, one at a time.
Then turn the egg mixture into the pan containing the
remaining liquid to be blended, and cook over low flame
for 1 to 2 minutes, stirring constantly, without allowing
to boil.

BEURRE MANIE

To make beurre manié: work together 1 tablespoon
butter and 1 tablespoon flour until well blended. Add
to the sauce, and cook, stirring constantly, for 1 minute,
or until sauce is thickened.

Beurre manié may be prepared in advance in larger
quantity, and wrapped in wax paper or placed in a
plastic box. It will keep at least two weeks in refrigerator.

Basic Sauces

From only two basic sauces, French cooks develop an
infinite variety of dishes. Once mastered, brown sauce
and Bechamel open the door to nearly all classic cuisine,
and all possible inventions of creative cooking. In fact,
many preparations of meat and fish mean basically the
making of one of these sauces as an integral part of the
dish. When the cook sprinkles the meat with flour, then
stirs in consommé or wine, adding herbs such as bay leaf
or thyme, she is making a brown sauce in which the meat
will cook. Brown sauce made in the "grande manière"

has always been practically impossible to prepare at home. It requires the previous preparation of stock, then the reducing of the stock to glaze or half-glaze, and then the making of the sauce itself. The housewife solves the problem by dispensing with glaze or half-glaze and using instead strong bouillon, consommé, or bouillon cubes. Canned beef consommé makes excellent brown sauce. The characteristic flavor of consommé fades away into the flavors of the other ingredients, leaving only that much of the taste which is part of the sauce.

BASIC BROWN SAUCE

2 tablesp. butter	1 small bay leaf
2 medium-size carrots, diced	2 tablesp. flour
	1 cup dry white wine
1 medium-size onion, chopped	1½ cups consommé
	1 tablesp. tomato paste
2 sprigs parsley	½ teasp. salt
pinch of thyme	¼ teasp. pepper

In small, heavy saucepan, melt butter. Add carrots, onions, parsley, thyme, and bay leaf. Cook over low flame, stirring constantly, until vegetables are golden brown. Stir in flour and cook until slightly brown. Stir in wine and consommé. Add tomato paste, salt, and pepper. Bring to boil. Cover and simmer for 30 minutes. Strain. Makes 2 cups.

Brown sauce may be prepared in advance and keeps well in refrigerator for more than two weeks.

BASIC BECHAMEL SAUCE

2 tablesp. butter	2½ cups hot milk
2 tablesp. chopped onions	½ teasp. salt
2 tablesp. flour	¼ teasp. white pepper
pinch of grated nutmeg	

In small, heavy saucepan, melt butter. As soon as butter is melted, add onions and cook over medium flame for 3 minutes, or until onions begin to turn golden. Stir in flour. Stir in milk and cook, stirring constantly until smooth. Add salt, pepper, and nutmeg, and cook over low flame for 30 minutes, stirring occasionally. Strain.

Makes 2 cups.

Bechamel sauce may be prepared in advance, and keeps well in refrigerator for more than two weeks.

SAUCE BLANCHE
(White Sauce)

2 tablesp. butter	½ teasp. salt
1 tablesp. flour	1 egg yolk
2 cups water	2 tablesp. lemon juice

Melt 1 tablespoon butter in small, heavy saucepan. Stir in flour. Add cold water and salt. Stir in egg yolk and cook over low flame, stirring briskly. Bring to boiling point, but do not boil. Take pan off fire and add remaining butter and lemon juice. Stir until well blended.

This sauce is served with boiled fish and boiled vegetables such as asparagus, cauliflower, and broccoli.

SAUCE BORDELAISE

This is one of the really great French sauces. It wonderfully enhances the flavor of meat and the bouquet of wine.

Serve it with the greatest red wine you can afford. A great wine, a steak Bordelaise with French-fried potatoes, followed by cheese with French bread (no salty crackers) , is a dinner to remember.

2 tablesp. finely chopped shallots (or scallions without tops)	¾ cup brown sauce
	½ teasp. lemon juice
	1 tablesp. butter, cut into small pieces
½ cup red Bordeaux wine	
pinch of freshly ground pepper	

In small, heavy saucepan, combine shallots (or scallions) , wine, and pepper. Bring to boil and simmer for 10 minutes, or until reduced to approximately 1 tablespoon of liquid. Stir in brown sauce and simmer for 10 minutes, or until reduced to approximately ½ cup. Strain. Off fire, add lemon juice and butter, stirring until well blended. Pour over meat.

Makes enough for 1 large or 4 individual steaks.

SAUCE BEARNAISE

In France, sauce Béarnaise is seldom made at home. French housewives are reluctant to make it because it is one of the hardest things to make successfully. Many dishes which seem difficult, such as soufflé, omelet, or puff paste, require only reasonable attention. Béarnaise is so sensitive that it will curdle at the drop of a piece of butter.

Americans probably won't try it for an added reason: shallots, one of the essential ingredients, are hard to come by in this country.

If you find shallots and feel like trying, by all means, do it. Many French people order "Chateaubriand," the luscious French steak, as much for its splendid companion, sauce Béarnaise, as for the steak itself.

So, we give here the recipe for the "happy few."

If you do make it, remember: It should be whisked briskly all the time; the pan should not be heated to boiling point; the butter should be added in small pieces and thoroughly blended each time before adding another piece.

¼ cup dry white wine
¼ cup white vinegar
2 shallots, chopped
4 peppercorn, crushed
3 egg yolks
¾ cup butter (1½ sticks)
½ teasp. salt
½ teasp. dried tarragon leaves
½ teasp. finely chopped parsley

In small, heavy saucepan, combine wine, vinegar, shallots, and peppercorns. Cook over brisk flame until liquid is reduced to approximately 2 tablespoons. In top of double boiler, combine egg yolks, 1 tablespoon butter, salt, and tarragon. Strain liquid from saucepan through a fine sieve into top of double boiler. Mix well. Place top over hot (but not boiling) water and cook, whipping constantly, until creamy. Gradually add remaining butter cut into small pieces, whipping constantly until smooth and well blended. Add parsley. Serve warm. (Béarnaise cannot be served hot because heating would cause it to curdle.) It should be the consistency of thick mayonnaise.

MADEIRA SAUCE

1 cup brown sauce
2 tablesp. chopped mushroom peelings or stems (optional)

¼ cup Madeira wine
pinch of freshly ground pepper

In small, heavy saucepan, combine brown sauce and mushroom peelings (if available). Bring to boil. Lower flame and cook, uncovered, over a very low flame for 15 minutes. Add Madeira wine and pepper. Cook until mixture is hot, but do not allow to boil.

To be used with red meat.

SAUCE MORNAY

1 tablesp. butter
1 tablesp. flour
1 cup milk

½ teasp. salt
2 tablesp. grated Swiss cheese

In small, heavy saucepan, melt butter. Stir in flour. Add milk and cook, stirring constantly, until it boils. Lower flame. Add cheese and cook, stirring constantly, for 5 minutes, or until smooth and well blended.

Sauce Mornay is mostly used with simply cooked fish. The fish is placed in a buttered heatproof dish, covered with a generous layer of Mornay sauce, and broiled under the flame of the broiler for 5 minutes, or until golden. It is served piping hot in the dish in which it has been broiled.

SAUCE PIQUANTE

1 tablesp. butter	½ cup dry white wine
2 tablesp. chopped onions	1 tablesp. wine vinegar
1 tablesp. flour	1 tablesp. dry mustard
½ cup consommé	1 medium-size pickle, thinly sliced

In small, heavy saucepan, heat butter. Add onions and cook until slightly browned. Sprinkle with flour. Stir in consommé, wine, and vinegar. Bring to boil. Add mustard and cook until smooth, stirring constantly. Simmer for 10 minutes, stirring occasionally. Correct seasoning. Add pickle and continue simmering for 5 minutes more.

Good with red meat, excellent with pork and tongue.

MAITRE D'HOTEL BUTTER

½ lb. butter	1 tablesp. finely chopped
½ teasp. salt	parsley
¼ teasp. white pepper	1 tablesp. lemon juice

In a mixing bowl, work butter with a wooden spoon until creamy. Add salt, pepper, parsley, and lemon juice. Mix well. Let stand in refrigerator for ½ hour.

Served mostly with boiled fish or with vegetables.

SAUCE POULETTE

2 tablesp. butter	¼ teasp. pepper
1 tablesp. flour	2 sprigs parsley
2 cups clear chicken broth	2 egg yolks
½ teasp. salt	juice of one lemon
1 tablesp. finely chopped parsley	

In medium-size heavy saucepan, heat 1 tablespoon butter. Add flour and cook for 1 minute, stirring constantly. Stir in chicken broth. Add salt, pepper, and sprigs of parsley. Bring to boil, stirring occasionally. Lower flame and simmer for 30 minutes. Discard sprigs of parsley. Blend sauce with yolks. Off fire, add lemon juice, chopped parsley, and remaining butter cut into small pieces. Stir until butter is melted and well blended. Serve hot.

Good with mussels, oysters, white meat, and vegetables.

HOLLANDAISE SAUCE

¼ lb. butter
1 teasp. arrowroot
5 tablesp. scalded milk, warm

pinch of salt
2 egg yolks
2 tablesp. lemon juice
pinch of freshly ground pepper

In top of double boiler, combine 1 tablespoon butter, arrowroot, milk, salt, and egg yolks. Stir with wire whip until well mixed. Place top over boiling water and whip until the mixture thickens. Remove top of double boiler and gradually add remaining butter cut into small pieces, whipping constantly, until smooth and well blended. Correct seasoning. Add lemon juice and pepper.

Good with white-meated fish or boiled vegetables.

MAYONNAISE

2 egg yolks
¼ teasp. salt

1 cup salad oil
½ teasp. lemon juice

Take eggs from refrigerator and let stand at room temperature for 1 hour before making mayonnaise.

In mixing bowl, break yolks and combine with salt. Very gradually add oil, beating constantly. When mixture thickens, add lemon juice. Keep in refrigerator.

According to taste, mustard, capers, parsley, or anchovies may be added singly or together.

AIOLI

"Aioli" is the name of a dish of hot boiled fish and vegetables served with a garlic mayonnaise. All white-meated fish may be used. In Provence, no aioli is considered complete if it does not include boiled snails (without shells).

In the northern part of France, "aioli" has taken the meaning of garlic mayonnaise only, and it is served much as plain mayonnaise, with cold fish, meat, or vegetables.

2 cloves garlic, crushed or pressed
2 egg yolks (at room temperature)
1 teasp. water
¼ teasp. salt
pinch of freshly ground pepper
1 cup olive oil

In mixing bowl, combine garlic, yolks, water, salt, and pepper. Very gradually, add oil, beating constantly until mixture thickens. Keep in refrigerator.

VELOUTE FOR POULTRY
(Sauce Supreme)

2 tablesp. butter
2 tablesp. flour
2 cups clear chicken broth
2 tablesp. chopped fresh mushrooms (or canned sliced mushrooms)
pinch of grated nutmeg
1 small bay leaf
pinch of thyme
½ teasp. salt
¼ teasp. white pepper
⅛ cup heavy cream
2 egg yolks

Heat butter in heavy saucepan. Stir in flour. Add chicken broth and cook, stirring constantly, until smooth. Add mushrooms, nutmeg, bay leaf, thyme, salt, and pepper. Cook over low flame, stirring occasionally, for 30 minutes. Add cream. Stir in yolks. Heat but do not allow to boil. Serve hot.

VELOUTE FOR FISH

2 tablesp. butter
2 tablesp. flour
1 cup bottled clam juice
1 cup water
2 tablesp. chopped fresh mushrooms (or canned sliced mushrooms)
pinch of grated nutmeg
pinch of thyme
1 small bay leaf
½ teasp. salt
¼ teasp. white pepper
⅛ cup heavy cream
2 egg yolks

Heat butter in heavy saucepan. Stir in flour. Add clam juice and water and cook, stirring constantly, until smooth. Add mushrooms, nutmeg, bay leaf, thyme, salt, and pepper. Cook over low flame, stirring occasionally, for 30 minutes. Add cream. Stir in yolks. Heat but do not allow to boil. Serve hot.

CAPER SAUCE

2 tablesp. butter	½ teasp. salt
1 tablesp. flour	1 egg yolk
2 cups water	2 tablesp. capers

In small, heavy saucepan, melt 1 tablespoon butter. Stir in flour. Add cold water and salt. Stir in egg yolk and cook over low flame, stirring constantly. Bring to boiling point but do not boil. Take pan off fire and add remaining butter and capers. Stir until well blended.

This sauce is served with boiled fish.

Chapter IX

Salads

Oᴺᴇ ᴏꜰ ᴛʜᴇ ɢʀᴇᴀᴛᴇsᴛ culinary surprises for French people visiting the United States, is to be served a salad with "French dressing"—and they usually don't like it much.

If there is such a thing as a "French dressing" it is "vinaigrette": salt, pepper, oil, and vinegar. This is the basic dressing for nearly all salads and the only dressing (with the possible addition of chopped herbs) for what is called "simple salads." "Simple salads" include green tossed salad and green vegetable salads.

"Salades composées," which are made of many different ingredients, are mostly served as hors-d'oeuvre. The dressing is more elaborate and often includes mayonnaise.

VINAIGRETTE
(basic dressing)

1 teasp. salt	1 tablesp. vinegar
¼ teasp. pepper	(preferably wine vinegar)
	3 tablesp. vegetable oil

In salad bowl, combine salt, pepper, and vinegar. Stir

until salt is dissolved. Stir in oil. Mix well. Add salad and
toss gently.

For a salad for 4 to 6 persons.

POTATO SALAD

Few Americans who have tasted potato salad in France
and found it delicious would guess of what ingredients
the dressing is made. The use of wine and consommé in
potato salad is so unexpected that, when they are told,
they think it is just a trimming, and unessential.

On the contrary, it is very important. Potatoes absorb
the flavoring of the seasoning when they are still warm—
otherwise they get a "cold potatoes" taste which pierces
through the dressing.

The problem is that when warm, potatoes absorb oil
so well that they become oily and lose the right consistency. Wine and consommé dilute the oil and vinegar,
keep the smoothness of the potatoes, and add their own
flavors which go perfectly with potatoes.

The best temperature at which to eat potato salad is
lukewarm. It may also be eaten cold, but is never kept in
the refrigerator.

8 medium-size potatoes	2 tablesp. consommé
1 teasp. salt	2 tablesp. dry white wine
1/2 teasp. freshly ground pepper	1/2 tablesp. dried tarragon leaves
1/4 cup wine vinegar	1 tablesp. chopped parsley
	1/2 cup oil

Cook potatoes in salted water for 30 minutes, or until
tender. Drain. Peel potatoes while still warm, and cut
into slices approximately 1/4 inch thick. Place in salad
bowl.

In another bowl, combine salt, pepper, vinegar, consommé, and wine. Mix until salt is dissolved. Add tarragon, parsley, and oil. Mix well. Pour over potatoes.
Toss gently but thoroughly until all liquid is absorbed.
Serve while still warm, or cold.

Serves 4.

WINE: *A light red wine:*
        Red Bordeaux; Beaujolais; domestic claret.
        Or a chilled dry white wine:
        Bordeaux Graves; Pouilly-Fuissé; white Côtes du
        Rhône; Alsatian Riesling; Pinot Blanc.
        Or a rosé wine.

SALAD MADRAS
(Rice Salad)

3 tomatoes	¼ teasp. pepper
2 green peppers	2 tablesp. salad oil
½ teasp. dry mustard	1 tablesp. wine vinegar
½ teasp. salt	2 cups cooked rice

Peel and slice tomatoes. Cut green peppers into strips,
approximately ⅛ inch wide.

In salad bowl, dissolve mustard in 1 teaspoon water.
Add salt and pepper. Stir in oil. Mix well. Add vinegar.
Add green peppers, tomatoes, and rice, tossing after each
addition. Let stand in refrigerator for ½ hour.

Serves 4.

WINE: *A chilled dry white wine:*
        Bordeaux Graves; Alsatian Riesling; Pouilly-
        Fuissé; French chablis; Pinot Blanc.

SALAD "SHEPHERDESS"

1 cup cooked rice	½ teasp. salt
4 hard-cooked eggs, sliced	¼ teasp. pepper
1 teasp. finely chopped	½ teasp. prepared
scallion	horseradish
2 tablesp. sour cream	

In salad bowl, combine eggs, rice, and scallion. In mixing bowl, combine salt, pepper, horseradish, and sour
cream. Blend well. Pour over rice mixture. Toss thoroughly but gently.

SPAGHETTI SALAD

Makes a fine hors-d'oeuvre or a delicious luncheon main dish.

These proportions are for a main dish.

¼ lb. spaghetti, broken into 2-inch pieces, cooked
2 tablesp. dry white wine
1 tablesp. wine vinegar
1 teasp. olive oil
¼ teasp. salt
pinch of pepper
1 stalk celery, thinly sliced

10-oz. package frozen artichokes, thawed and quartered
¼ cup mayonnaise
1 tablesp. tomato paste
2 hard-cooked eggs
2 tablesp. chopped parsley
¼ lb. cooked ham, coarsely chopped (or leftover chicken)

Keep spaghetti lukewarm.

In a bowl combine wine, vinegar, oil, salt, and pepper. Add celery and artichokes. Let stand ½ hour, turning occasionally.

Meanwhile, combine mayonnaise and tomato paste. Stir well. Separate yolks and whites of hard-cooked eggs and chop separately.

In heated mixing bowl, combine spaghetti and mayonnaise mixture. Mix well. Add celery and artichokes. Toss gently. Correct seasoning.

For serving: Put salad in a large salad bowl. With a spatula arrange salad in dome shape. Arrange parsley, chopped yolks, chopped egg whites, and ham (or leftover chicken) on top of salad.

Serves 4 to 6.

WINE: *A chilled white wine:*
DRY: Bordeaux Graves; Alsatian Riesling or Traminer; Sauvignon Blanc.
SWEET: Bordeaux Sauternes; Gewurztraminer; sweet Semillon.

DRIED BEANS SALAD

2 cups cooked dried beans
½ medium-size onion, thinly sliced

6 tablesp. vinaigrette
1 tablesp. chopped parsley

Drain beans and keep lukewarm. Separate onion rings. In salad bowl, combine vinaigrette, beans, and parsley. Toss gently, but thoroughly. Decorate with onion rings. Serve cold.

Serves 4.

LENTIL SALAD

2 cups cooked lentils
6 tablesp. vinaigrette

3 anchovy filets, cut into small pieces

Drain lentils. Keep lukewarm. In salad bowl, combine vinaigrette, lentils, and anchovies. Toss gently but thoroughly. Serve cold.

Serves 4.

STRING BEAN SALAD

2 cups cooked string beans   4 tablesp. vinaigrette

Drain string beans and cool. In salad bowl, combine vinaigrette and string beans. Mix well.

Serves 4.

TOMATO SALAD

4 tomatoes, peeled and sliced
4 tablesp. vinaigrette

1 tablesp. finely chopped onion

1 tablesp. chopped parsley

In salad bowl, combine vinaigrette, tomatoes, and onions. Mix well. Sprinkle with parsley.

Serves 4.

BEET SALAD

1 cup cooked (or canned) beets, sliced
½ teasp. salt
¼ teasp. pepper

1 teasp. prepared mustard
1 teasp. wine vinegar
2 tablesp. oil
1 teasp. chopped parsley

In mixing bowl, combine salt, pepper, mustard, and vinegar. Stir until mustard is dissolved. Add oil. Mix.

Add beets. Mix well. Arrange in serving dish. Sprinkle with parsley.
Serves 4.

CUCUMBER SALAD

1 cucumber   4 tablesp. vinaigrette
           1 tablesp. finely chopped parsley

Peel cucumber and cut into paper-thin slices. In salad bowl, combine vinaigrette, cucumbers, and chopped parsley. Toss.
Serves 4.

LEEK SALAD

"Leek salad" is called in France "the poor-man's asparagus"—but there are many who prefer it to the "rich man's" variety. It is fresh and delicious.

6 large leeks   4 tablesp. vinaigrette
           1 tablesp. chopped parsley

Cut leeks in four, lengthwise. Wash thoroughly until no sand remains between leaves. Cook in salted boiling water for 30 minutes, or until leeks are very tender.
Place leeks in salad bowl. Pour vinaigrette over leeks. Sprinkle with parsley. Serve warm or cold.
Serves 4.

SHRIMP SALAD DEAUVILLE

2 cups shrimps, cooked and   1 tablesp. vinegar
  shelled   1 teasp. prepared mustard
½ cup halved walnuts   ¾ teasp. salt
1 apple, sliced   pinch of cayenne pepper
3 hard-cooked eggs, halved   2 tablesp. vegetable oil
1 cup canned mushrooms,   1 tablesp. minced celery
  drained   1 tablesp. mayonnaise
1 cup shredded iceberg
  lettuce

In salad bowl, arrange shrimps, walnuts, apple, eggs, mushrooms, and lettuce.

In mixing bowl, combine vinegar, mustard, salt, cayenne pepper, oil, celery, and mayonnaise. Mix thoroughly. Pour over salad.

Serves 4 to 6.

WINE: *A chilled white wine:*

DRY: Bordeaux Graves; Alsatian Riesling or Traminer; Sáuvignon Blanc.

SWEET: Bordeaux Sauternes; Gewurztraminer; sweet Semillon.

BEEF SALAD

1 cup leftover beef, thinly sliced	2 tablesp. wine vinegar
	4 tablesp. vegetable oil
6 medium-size potatoes, boiled and sliced	1/2 teasp. dried tarragon leaves
4 tomatoes, peeled and sliced	1 tablesp. chopped parsley
1 teasp. salt	2 hard-cooked eggs, sliced
1/4 teasp. pepper	

In salad bowl, combine beef, potatoes, and tomatoes.

In mixing bowl, combine salt, pepper, vinegar, oil, and tarragon. Mix well. Pour over salad. Sprinkle with parsley. Decorate with egg slices.

Serves 4.

WINE: *A light red wine:*
Red Bordeaux; Beaujolais; domestic claret.
Or a chilled dry white wine:
Bordeaux Graves; Pouilly-Fuissé; white Côtes du Rhône; Alsatian Riesling; Pinot Blanc.
Or a rosé wine.

Chapter X

Vegetables

THE FRENCH don't like vegetables. This is why they make them taste so good. As with fish (and for the same reason), the ingenuity of French cooking has found many ways to make vegetables more appetizing and tastier.

Plain boiled vegetables are regarded in France as fit only for diets, with the exception of boiled potatoes, which go so wonderfully with the luscious sauce dishes of French cuisine.

Cooked in the French manner, a vegetable is not only an accompaniment to the main dish, but is a delicious dish in itself.

ARTICHOKES CASSEROLE

1 10-oz. package frozen artichokes	¼ teasp. freshly ground pepper
3 tablesp. olive oil	2 tablesp. vinegar
2 tablesp. finely chopped onions	¼ cup dry white wine
½ teasp. salt	½ cup boiling water
	1 clove garlic, crushed
	½ bay leaf, crushed

1 tablesp. beurre manié

In large, heavy skillet, heat oil. Add onions and frozen artichokes. Cook over moderate flame, turning frequently, for 5 minutes, or until the artichokes are separated and the onions are softened but not browned. Add salt, pepper, vinegar, and wine. Bring to boil and cook over high flame for 10 minutes, or until liquid is reduced to about 2 tablespoons. Add boiling water, garlic, and bay leaf. Cover and cook over low flame for 30 minutes. Remove artichokes to heated serving dish and keep warm. Add beurre manié to liquid in skillet. Cook for 5 minutes. Pour over artichokes. Serve hot.

Serves 4.

ARTICHOKES A LA GRECQUE

1 cup water	3 peppercorns
1 10-oz. package frozen artichokes	pinch of thyme
	pinch of fennel seeds
3 tablesp. lemon juice	pinch of coriander seeds
¼ cup olive oil	1 small bay leaf
½ teasp. salt	

In large, heavy skillet, cook artichokes in boiling water for 5 minutes, or until they are separated. Add all remaining ingredients. Bring to boil. Cover and simmer for 20 minutes. Cool in cooking liquid. Serve artichokes with 4 tablespoon liquid.

Serves 4.

ASPARAGUS

Asparagus is prepared in France exactly as it is in America: it is cooked in salted boiling water for 10 to 15 minutes, according to size. It is served hot or cold.

Serve hot with sauce Blanche* or maître d'hôtel butter.**

Serve cold with plain mayonnaise or mayonnaise whipped with heavy cream in the proportion of 2 tablespoons heavy cream for ½ cup mayonnaise.

* Recipe given on page 125.
** Recipe given on page 130.

STRING BEANS "POULETTE"

1 lb. string beans   ½ cup sauce Poulette*

Remove stems and tips from beans. Wash and place in a saucepan. Cook in salted boiling water for 15 minutes, or until beans are tender. Drain thoroughly. Add sauce Poulette. Mix well. Serve hot.

Serves 4.

RED BEANS IN WINE

4 cups red beans, cooked   1 tablesp. flour
1 tablesp. butter   ¾ cups red wine
1 onion, chopped   ¼ cup consommé

In Dutch oven or large saucepan, heat butter. Add onion and cook until slightly browned. Add flour and cook until flour is slightly browned. Stir in wine. Add beans and consommé. Bring to boil. Cover and simmer for 30 minutes. Correct seasoning. Serve hot.

Serves 4.

LOUBIA
(Dried Beans)

An appetizing way of cooking dried beans comes from North Africa. It is an Arabian dish adopted by the French "colons." Its exotic flavor is not too exotic for French palates and yet it has that special touch which makes a new treat of an old and overused vegetable.

Served with meatballs and accompanied by a good unpretentious red French regional wine or a domestic wine, it makes a delectable family dish. Presented casserole style, it is an original and elegant buffet dish.

1 lb. marrow beans   ¼ cup tomato sauce
2 tablesp. olive oil   2 tablesp. tomato paste
2 tablesp. chopped onions   1 teasp. cumin seeds
1 clove garlic, crushed   pinch of cayenne pepper
  (optional)   2 tablesp. chopped parsley

* Recipe given on page 130.

Cook beans according to directions on package. Drain. In large saucepan, heat the oil. Add onions and cook until slightly browned. Add tomato sauce, tomato paste, cumin, pepper, and beans. Mix gently. Cover and simmer for 10 minutes. Correct seasoning. Sprinkle with parsley. Serve hot.

Serves 4 to 6.

WINE: *A red wine:*

Red Bordeaux; French red Burgundy; red Côtes du Rhône; domestic claret or Burgundy.

BRAISED CABBAGE

2 medium-size cabbages
½ lb. salt pork, cut into thin slices
1 carrot, sliced
1 onion studded with 2 cloves
1 sprig parsley
1 bay leaf
pinch of thyme
2 cups consommé

Cut cabbages in quarters. Remove hard cores. Wash and cook in boiling salted water for 15 minutes. Drain and let stand in cold water for 10 minutes. Drain. Remove thick, hard ribs at base of leaves. Press cabbage between hands until all water is squeezed out. Line bottom of Dutch oven or heavy saucepan with slices of salt pork. Add carrot, onion, parsley, bay leaf, thyme, and cabbage. Cover with remaining slices of salt pork. Add consommé. Bring to boil. Cover and simmer gently for 2 hours. Serve hot.

Serves 4.

Serve with cooked garlic sausage or Polish-style sausage.

CARROTS VICHY

1 lb. carrots, scraped and cut into slices ½ inch thick
2 tablesp. butter, cut into small pieces
2 cups water
1 teasp. granulated sugar
¼ teasp. salt
1 teasp. chopped parsley

In heavy saucepan, combine carrots, butter, water, sugar and salt. Cover. Bring to boil. Lower flame and simmer for 30 minutes. Shake carrots gently into pan, and continue cooking, shaking carrots occasionally, for 20 minutes more, or until they are golden brown. Sprinkle with parsley. Serve hot.

Serves 4.

CAULIFLOWER AU GRATIN

1 medium-size cauliflower	1/4 teasp. pepper
2 tablesp. butter	pinch of grated nutmeg
1 tablesp. flour	2 tablesp. grated Swiss
2 cups scalded milk	cheese
1/2 teasp. salt	1/4 cup fresh bread crumbs

Trim cauliflower, separate the flowers, and wash in salted cold water. Cook in boiling salted water for 12 to 15 minutes, or until tender but not soft. Drain.

Meanwhile, in small, heavy saucepan, melt 1 tablespoon butter. Add flour. Stir in milk. Add salt, pepper, nutmeg, and cheese. Cook over low flame, stirring constantly until smooth. Arrange cauliflower in ovenproof, buttered dish. Cover with cheese mixture. Sprinkle with bread crumbs. Dot with remaining butter. Broil under broiler flame until browned. Serve hot.

Serves 4.

BRAISED CELERY

6 stalks celery	1 cup consommé
1 small-size onion, sliced	1 tablesp. beurre manié
1 medium-size carrot, sliced	

Wash and trim celery. Cut each stalk into 2 pieces. Cook in boiling salted water for 5 minutes. Drain.

In large, heavy saucepan, combine onion and carrot. Place celery on top. Add consommé. Bring to boil. Cover and simmer for 1 hour, or until celery is tender. Remove celery to heated serving dish and keep warm. Discard onion and carrot. Cook liquid in pan over brisk flame until reduced to ½ cup. Add beurre manié to pan. Cook for 3 minutes, or until sauce thickens. Pour over celery. Serve hot.

Serves 4 to 6.

CELERY MORNAY

6 stalks celery, cleaned and trimmed	2 tablesp. grated Swiss cheese
1 cup sauce Mornay*	2 tablesp. bread crumbs
3 tablesp. melted butter	

Cut each stalk of celery into two pieces. Cook in salted boiling water for 45 minutes. Drain thoroughly.

Cover bottom of ovenproof dish with ½ cup of sauce Mornay. Place celery over sauce. Sprinkle with grated cheese. Cover with remaining sauce Mornay. Sprinkle with bread crumbs. Pour melted butter over crumbs. Broil under broiler flame until top is well browned. Serve hot.

Serves 4 to 6.

EGGPLANT MEUNIERE

1 large eggplant	¼ cup flour
1 teasp. salt	¼ cup butter
2 tablesp. chopped parsley	

Peel eggplant and cut into slices ½ inch thick. Place in a bowl. Sprinkle with salt and let stand for 30 minutes. Pat dry with paper towel. Dredge with flour.

In large skillet, heat 2 tablespoons butter. Add eggplant and cook over brisk flame for 10 minutes on each side, or until well browned. Remove eggplant to heated serving dish. Sprinkle with parsley. Keep warm.

Add remaining butter to skillet and cook until butter is slightly browned. Pour over eggplant. Serve very hot.

Serves 4.

With rice this makes a tasty lunch or Lenten dinner.

* Recipe given on page 129.

PEAS A LA FRANÇAISE

2 cups shelled peas
(fresh, frozen, or canned)
6 lettuce leaves
6 small white onions
1½ teasp. granulated sugar

2 sprigs parsley
3 tablesp. butter
1 teasp. salt
½ teasp. pepper
½ cup water

In saucepan, combine peas, lettuce, onions, sugar, parsley, 2 tablespoons butter, salt, and pepper. Mix well. Let stand for 1 hour. Just before cooking, add water. Cover and bring to boil. Then cook briskly for 25 minutes, when the liquid in the pan should be reduced to approximately 2 tablespoons. Remove pan from fire and add 1 tablespoon butter. Do not stir, but roll pan gently until butter is melted.

Serves 4.

MUSHROOMS NICOISE

12 large mushroom caps
1 1-lb.-12-oz. can tomatoes,
drained and mashed
½ teasp. salt

¼ teasp. pepper
2 tablesp. vegetable oil
1 tablesp. chopped parsley
6 black olives, pitted

Wash and drain mushrooms. Arrange in greased baking dish. Bake at 350° F. for 5 minutes.

Fill mushrooms with tomatoes. Add salt and pepper. Sprinkle with oil. Continue baking for 15 minutes more. Sprinkle with parsley. Garnish with olives.

Serves 4.

Serve: hot, with red meat;
cold, with cold cuts;
hot or cold, as an hors-d'oeuvre.

SPINACH AU GRATIN

2 lbs. spinach
2 tablesp. butter
¼ teasp. pepper
½ teasp. salt
pinch of grated nutmeg
pinch of granulated sugar

1 teasp. flour
⅓ cup light cream
⅓ cup sauce Mornay*
1 tablesp. grated Swiss
cheese
2 tablesp. melted butter

* Recipe given on page 129.

Clean and trim spinach. In large, heavy saucepan, melt 1 tablespoon butter. Add spinach and cook over brisk flame for 5 minutes, stirring constantly. Remove pan from fire. Add pepper, salt, nutmeg, and sugar. Sprinkle with flour. Mix well. Return pan to fire and cook for 2 minutes, stirring constantly. Again remove pan from fire. Stir in cream. Return pan to fire and bring to boil, stirring constantly. Lower flame. Cover and simmer for 20 minutes. Off fire, add remaining butter cut into small pieces, stirring until butter is melted and well blended.

In bottom of ovenproof dish, spread 3 tablespoons of sauce Mornay. Add spinach. Cover with remaining sauce Mornay. Sprinkle with grated cheese, Add melted butter. Bake at 500° F. for 3 minutes, or until the top is golden. Serve hot.

Serves 4.

CREAMED SPINACH

2 lbs. spinach	pinch of grated nutmeg
2 tablesp. butter	pinch of granulated sugar
½ teasp. salt	1 teasp. flour
¼ teasp. pepper	⅓ cup light cream

Clean and trim spinach. In saucepan, melt 1 tablespoon butter. Add spinach, and cook over brisk flame for 5 minutes, stirring constantly. Remove pan from fire. Add salt, pepper, nutmeg, and sugar. Sprinkle with flour. Mix well. Return pan to fire and cook for 2 minutes, stirring constantly. Again remove pan from fire. Stir in cream. Return pan to fire and bring to boil, stirring constantly. Lower flame. Cover and simmer for 20 minutes. Remove pan from fire. Add remaining butter, cut into small pieces, stirring until butter is melted and well blended. Serve hot.

Serves 4.

TOMATOES PROVENÇAL

6 medium-size tomatoes	1 clove garlic, finely
¼ cup olive oil	chopped
1 teasp. salt	3 tablesp. parsley, finely
¼ teasp. freshly ground	chopped
pepper	½ cup fresh bread crumbs

Cut tomatoes in half. In large skillet, heat oil. Add tomatoes, cut side down, and cook for 10 minutes. Turn tomatoes and cook other side for 10 minutes. Remove tomatoes to baking dish. Reserve cooking oil. Salt and pepper tomatoes. Sprinkle with garlic and parsley. Cover with bread crumbs. Sprinkle with reserved oil from skillet. Bake at 400° F. for 30 minutes, or until top is well browned. Serve hot.

Serves 4.

"Tomatoes Provençal" is delicious served with red meat, especially with lamb.

With rice or an omelet, and a green salad, it makes a tasty Lenten or summer dinner.

POTATOES LYONNAISE

2 lbs. potatoes, boiled	¼ teasp. pepper
and peeled	2 large onions, thinly sliced
¼ cup butter	1 tablesp. parsley
½ teasp. salt	

Cut potatoes into slices ¼ inch thick. In heavy skillet, heat 2 tablespoons butter. Add potatoes, salt, and pepper, and cook over medium flame for 20 minutes, shaking potatoes in pan approximately every 5 minutes. Meanwhile, heat remaining butter in small skillet. Add onions and cook until slightly browned. Add onions to potatoes. Mix well and continue cooking for 10 minutes, shaking potato mixture in pan occasionally. Sprinkle with parsley. Serve hot.

Serves 4.

GRATIN DAUPHINOIS
(Gratin of Potatoes)

8 medium-size potatoes	1 cup scalded milk
½ teasp. salt	1 cup light cream
¼ teasp. white pepper	1 egg, beaten
pinch of grated nutmeg	¼ cup grated Swiss cheese

Peel potatoes and cut into slices approximately ¼ inch thick. In a bowl, combine potatoes, salt, pepper, nutmeg, milk, cream, egg, and grated cheese. Turn mixture into a buttered baking dish. Dot with butter. Bake at 400° F. for 1 hour, or until potatoes are tender and top is browned. Serve hot.

Serves 4.

POTATOES "PERSILLEES"

8 medium-size potatoes, peeled and cut in halves	¼ teasp. pepper
	3 tablesp. chopped parsley
½ cup water	2 tablesp. butter, cut into small pieces
½ cup consommé	
1 teasp. salt	

In buttered baking dish, combine potatoes, water, consommé, salt, pepper, 2 tablespoons parsley, and butter. Cover with aluminum foil. Bake at 400° F. for 1 hour, or until potatoes are tender and liquid is reduced to approximately half of the original volume. Sprinkle with parsley. Serve hot.

Serves 4.

RICE MALGACHE

2 tablesp. lard	1 teasp. salt
2 tablesp. chopped scallion	pinch of saffron
1 green pepper, coarsely chopped	1 cup consommé
	2 cups boiling water
1 cup Carolina rice	

In large heavy saucepan, heat lard. Add scallion and pepper. Cook until browned. Add rice and cook, stirring

constantly, until rice is well coated with fat. Add salt,
saffron, consommé, and water. Bring to boil. Cover and
simmer for 15 minutes, or until rice has absorbed all
liquid. Serve hot.

Serves 4 to 6.

MACARONI

Macaroni was born in Italy, but France adopted it
when it was still in its infancy. It is an integral part of
French cuisine, and has been used for centuries everywhere in France.

French recipes are different from the traditional Italian ones—not so much because the tastes of the two countries differ, but rather because the French soil is richer
and the climate milder and, therefore, a greater variety
of ingredients are available.

"Macaroni au gratin" and "spaghetti timbales" are
as French as "soupe à l'oignon" or "crêpes Suzette," and,
in their way, they are as good.

MACARONI AU GRATIN

1 lb. macaroni	1¼ cups Bechamel sauce*
	2 tablesp. grated Swiss cheese

Cook macaroni in boiling salted water for 15 minutes,
or until done. Drain.

Butter an ovenproof casserole. Sprinkle bottom with
1 tablespoon grated cheese. Add ¼ cup Bechamel sauce.
Add layer of half macaroni. Cover with ½ cup Bechamel
sauce. Add second layer of remaining macaroni. Cover
with remaining Bechamel sauce. Sprinkle with remaining grated cheese. Dot with butter. Broil under flame of
broiler for 5 minutes, or until top is browned. Serve hot.

Serves 4.

* Recipe given on page 127.

SPAGHETTI TIMBALES

Timbales are served as a main dish, or with a light meat dish. These proportions are for timbales as a main dish.

1 lb. spaghetti, cooked
1 cup tomato sauce
2 tomatoes, peeled and quartered
⅛ cup Madeira wine
2 thin slices cooked ham, coarsely chopped

2 slices cooked tongue cut into small pieces
⅛ cup canned sliced mushrooms
⅛ cup grated Swiss cheese

In saucepan, combine spaghetti, tomato sauce, and tomatoes. Cook for 15 minutes. Add Madeira wine, ham, tongue, and mushrooms. Mix well, and cook for 10 minutes. Off fire, add grated cheese. Mix well.

Turn mixture into ovenproof casserole and bake at 450° F. for 10 minutes. Serve hot.

Serves 4.

WINE: *A chilled dry white wine:*
        Bordeaux Graves; French chablis; Pouilly-Fuissé; white Côtes du Rhône.

Chapter XI

Pastry and Desserts

SOME French sweet desserts are among the greatest: "Crêpes Suzette" or "Cherries Jubilee" are now a necessary item on first-class restaurant menus all over the world.

It seems odd, therefore, that French people do not regard sweet desserts as really part of "grande cuisine." Sweet dishes are served only on special occasions, or to complete a light dinner. The preferred way to end a meal is with a large tray of many varieties of cheeses, and then a bowl of seasonal fruits.

Cheese, without which no French meal is perfect, is served with bread and butter—no salty crackers, which take away from the flavors of the cheese and of the wine. Cheese is good with all kinds of bread: French bread, rye, pumpernickel, toast—and it would be a very poor wine which would not taste wonderful with cheese.

Preparation of Butter for Pastry

Most of the recipes for pastry call for butter worked until soft and all the water is removed.

This can be achieved by working the butter with a wooden spoon, but the best way is to place the butter on a floured towel, fold the towel over butter and knead until no more water appears on the butter.

Brioche and Croissant

No wonder French people see "la vie en rose." Wouldn't you if you began the day as they do with a huge cup of "café au lait" and an assortment of oven-warm brioches and croissants, not to mention the usual trimmings of fresh butter, jam, marmelade, and honey.

Brioche and croissant are seldom made at home. They are more often bought from bakers, who all make excellent ones. But rather than do without them, when they are not available French cooks will try their hand at making them.

This requires time, not that the actual working time is long, but both doughs are prepared in many steps, with long intervals between each step.

What makes the recipes a little difficult to follow is that the "tour-de-main" (know-how) is hard to grasp when explained. It is extremely simple when you have seen it done.

The encouraging side of it is that the doughs are delectable in themselves, and that even if your brioches or croissants don't look like much, that will not prevent them from being delicious.

The only trick with brioche is in the kneading of the dough. In fact, it is more a beating than a kneading, and the fluffiness and smoothness of the brioche is in direct relationship to the amount of "elbow grease" spent in this operation.

To give a good beating to the dough, take it well in hand by one end, lift it, and without loosening your grasp smack it on the floured board. Then take it by the other end and do the same thing, over and over again. It can well be compared to the paddling washerwomen used to give to linen, the dough being handled as the paddle was. Although we said that it takes a lot of elbow grease, the stroke actually comes from the wrist and not from the elbow or the shoulder.

Brioches, when you make them yourself, should be listed in the category of no-calorie foods, because you lose in the making as many calories as you gain in the eating. But there is nothing quite as elegant and delicious for breakfast.

BRIOCHE

1 cake yeast	1 tablesp. granulated
4 cups sifted flour	sugar
½ teasp. salt	1 cup butter
¼ cup milk	6 eggs

Soften yeast in ¼ cup warm water. In a bowl, mix yeast with 1 cup flour. Shape into a ball. Cover bowl and let stand in a warm place for 30 minutes.

Meanwhile, place remaining flour in a mixing bowl. Make a well in center of flour. Place salt, sugar, milk, eggs, and ½ cup butter in well. Work together with fingers, bringing flour gradually towards center. Lift dough with hand and beat it on a floured board until resilient. Cut remaining butter into small pieces and gradually work butter into dough, but working dough as little as possible. When well blended, add flour and yeast mixture from bowl, working gently with fingertips.

Shape dough into a ball and place in bowl. Cover bowl and let stand at room temperature for 4 hours, or until dough has doubled its volume. Punch down dough, which will then return to its original volume. Keep overnight in refrigerator.

When ready to use, punch dough again. Shape dough according to shape of mold (special brioche mold, loaf pan, ring, etc.), and fill generously buttered mold no more than two-thirds full. Let stand for 30 minutes, or until dough rises and reaches rim of mold. Brush with melted butter and bake at 450° F. for approximately 15 minutes, or until brioche is browned, and a cake-tester or pointed knife inserted in center comes out clean.

CROISSANT

2 yeast cakes	½ teasp. salt
¼ cup lukewarm water	1 tablesp. sugar
4 cups sifted flour	1½ cups milk
¾ lb. butter	

Dissolve yeast in water. Stir in one cup of flour and shape into a ball. With knife, cut a cross on the top of ball. Cover with towel and let stand in warm place until doubled in volume. Meanwhile, place remaining flour on board. Add salt and sugar. Make well in center and add milk, working dough until smooth. Add raised dough and mix well. Shape dough into ball. Cover with towel and let stand for 15 minutes. Roll out dough into rectangle about ½ inch thick.

Work butter until smooth and all water is removed. Shape butter into a square and place it on center of dough. Fold both ends of dough over center, one on top of the other. Roll out dough and fold again, both ends over center. Turn dough around. Roll out dough and fold again in the same manner. Keep dough overnight in refrigerator.

When ready to use, give dough a turn. (We use the expression a "turn," to mean the whole operation of rolling, folding, turning, and again rolling and folding.) Let stand in refrigerator for 1 hour. Roll out dough ⅛ inch thick and cut into 6 squares. Cut squares diagonally making 12 triangles. Starting from the base, roll up each triangle loosely. Give the roll the shape of a crescent by turning in both ends of roll. Place crescents on baking sheet. Cover with towel and let stand in warm place for about 1 hour, or until they have doubled in volume. Brush with milk or beaten egg and bake at 350° F. for 30 minutes, or until browned.

PUFF PASTE

You can't miss in making puff paste if you are very careful about the following points:

1. The butter should have exactly the same consistency as the dough. If the butter is softer, keep it in the refrigerator a little longer. If the dough is softer, take the butter out of the refrigerator and let it soften a little.

2. To make the flour and water mixture, use a wooden spoon or a fork, or mix with fingertips. The important thing is that it should be worked as little as possible.

3. Flour board lightly. If the dough is covered with too much flour, shake it off.

4. Roll the dough lightly. Avoid letting the butter break through the dough.

5. For the same reason, roll dough from center to edges without pressing on edges.

½ lb. butter	½ teasp. salt
2 cups flour	½ cup ice water

Work butter until it is soft and all water is removed. Keep in refrigerator.

In mixing bowl, sift flour and add salt and water. Combine working mixture as little as possible in order to make a stiff ball. Let dough stand in refrigerator for 20 minutes.

Place dough on floured board and roll into a rectangle approximately ½″ thick. Shape butter into square ½ inch thick. Place butter in center of dough. Fold both ends of rectangle over center, one on top of the other, covering the butter. Let stand in refrigerator for 20 minutes.

Roll out dough from center to edge into a rectangle 15″ by 8″ and ½″ thick. Fold in thirds. Turn dough around so that the shorter edge faces you. Roll out and fold dough again in the same manner.

Let stand in refrigerator for 20 minutes. Make two more "turns,"* with an interval of 20 minutes in re-

* See page 158 for definition of a "turn."

frigerator between turns. After last turn, leave in refrigerator for 20 minutes, or until ready to use.

Cooking time: This depends on the thickness of the paste which is baked for each specific shell or pastry, etc. For paste rolled ¼ inch thick, bake at 450° F. for 5 minutes. Reduce heat to 375° F. and continue baking for 30 minutes.

PIE CRUST

2 cups flour	4 tablesp. lard,
4 tablesp. butter,	soft but not liquid
soft but not liquid	½ teasp. salt
	½ cup ice water

Sift flour in mixing bowl. Make a well in center of flour. Place butter, lard, and salt in the well. Mix together with a pastry blender or a fork, adding water, a little at a time, just enough to gather the dough together. Shape dough into ball and wrap it in wax paper. Let stand in refrigerator for at least 2 hours. (It will keep 1 week in refrigerator.) When ready to use, roll out dough very thin on a floured board. Do not grease baking pan.

CREAM PUFFS

1 cup water	1 teasp. granulated sugar
½ cup butter, cut	1 cup sifted flour
into small pieces	5 eggs
½ teasp. salt	

In heavy saucepan, combine water, butter, salt, and sugar. Bring to boil. Remove pan from fire and add flour at once. Stir briskly with a wooden spoon until dough is smooth. Return pan to fire and cook, stirring constantly, until dough leaves the sides of the pan and forms a ball. Remove pan from fire and add eggs, one at a time, mixing after each one has been added. Spoon dough onto a greased baking sheet and bake at 375° F. for 45 minutes, or until puffs are dry and golden. Cool. Split puffs horizontally and fill with ice cream, whipped cream, or crème pâtissière.

WINE: Chilled champagne; chilled Bordeaux Sauternes; sweet Semillon.

SAVARIN

Savarin is less known in America than babas, although it is nearly the same thing. The only difference is that for babas, raisins and currants are added to the dough, and babas are baked in small molds instead of a large ring. Few people have the right kind of baba molds and anyway, as a dessert a large Savarin is much more attractive than small babas, which seem more appropriate for restaurants. Savarin may be decorated with pieces of candied fruits.

2 cups flour	4 eggs
1 envelope active dry yeast	⅔ cup butter
	2 tablesp. sugar
½ cup lukewarm milk	½ teasp. salt

Sift flour in mixing bowl. Dissolve yeast in milk, and stir in flour. Beat eggs lightly and add to dough, working dough until smooth. Add butter and continue working until well blended. Cover bowl and let stand in a warm place for 30 minutes. Add sugar and salt to dough and work until well blended. Butter generously a large ring mold and fill not more than ⅔ full with dough. Let stand for 1 hour, or until dough rises and reaches rim of mold. Bake at 400° F. for 15 minutes, or until browned. Unmold while hot. While still warm, pour rum syrup over it. Serve cold.

WINE: Chilled champagne; chilled Bordeaux Sauternes; sweet Semillon.

RUM SYRUP

½ cup sugar	1 tablesp. lemon juice
¾ cup water	3 tablesp. Jamaica rum

In small, heavy saucepan, combine sugar and water. Bring to boil and continue boiling for 5 minutes, stirring constantly. Remove from fire. When syrup is lukewarm, add lemon juice and rum. Pour over Savarin.

PAIN D'EPICES
(Spiced Cake)

2 cups flour	1 teasp. anisette
½ cup granulated sugar	1 teasp. rum
1 teasp. baking soda	1 teasp. ground cinnamon
1 cup milk	2 tablesp. liquid honey
½ cup blanched almonds	

In mixing bowl, combine flour, sugar, soda, milk, anisette, rum, and cinnamon. Work with wooden spoon until smooth. Cover and let stand overnight at room temperature. When ready to cook, stir in honey and almonds. Turn dough into buttered loaf pan (8"x5"x3"), no more than ½ full. Cover with aluminum foil. Bake at 400° F. for 15 minutes. Reduce heat to 350° and continue baking for 45 minutes. Unmold while hot. Serve cold, cut into thin slices. (For a special treat, spread the slices with butter.)

Pain d'epices keeps a few weeks in wax paper and aluminum foil.

CREPES SUZETTE

Crêpes Suzette are not difficult to make. They are only expensive! But they are well worth the cost. It is a perfect party dessert. The crêpes can be prepared in advance (even a day before), and kept in the refrigerator, making it easier for the hostess. Regardless of when they were made, the last operation always takes place in a chafing dish at the table. Then, the blazing of the crêpes is a dramatic show, the aroma of the flaming liquors makes the mouth water, and the crêpes themselves are a delicious treat that more than comes up to all the promises of the elaborate preparation.

Crêpes

1⅛ cups flour	3 eggs, beaten
4½ tablesp. granulated	1½ cups milk
sugar	1 tablesp. melted butter
pinch of salt	1½ tablesp. brandy

In deep bowl, sift flour, sugar, and salt. Combine beaten eggs and milk and stir into flour and sugar mixture until smooth. Add melted butter and brandy. Let stand for 2 hours.

In a frying pan 5 to 5½ inches across, heat 1 tablespoon butter. When butter is hot, pour in 1 full tablespoon of batter. Rotate pan quickly to spread batter. Cook for 1 minute on one side. Flip over and cook for 1 minute on other side. Pile crêpes flat, one on top of the other.

Crêpes Suzette

6 lumps sugar	1 tablesp. lemon juice
1 orange rind	3 tablesp. curacao
½ cup butter	3 tablesp. grand marnier
juice of 1 orange	½ cup cognac

Rub lumps of sugar on rind of orange. Crush sugar with butter and mix well with fork until mixture is creamy. In chafing dish, melt sugar and butter mixture. Add orange juice, lemon juice, curaçao, and grand marnier. Bring to boil. Lift crêpes into sauce. Heat crêpes, turning once and spooning sauce over them. Fold each crêpe in quarters and sprinkle with cognac. As soon as cognac is warm, ignite, and serve while sauce is flaming. Serve crêpes on heated plate with sauce over them.

Serves 4.

WINE: Chilled champagne

CREME RENVERSEE
(Caramel Custard)

2 cups milk	5 tablesp. granulated sugar
1 piece vanilla bean	3 eggs
	1 tablesp. water

Scald milk, with a piece of vanilla bean added. In mixing bowl, beat together eggs and 2½ tablespoons sugar for 1 minute. Stir in boiling milk, beating constantly until well blended.

Meanwhile, in small, heavy saucepan, cook remaining sugar with water, stirring constantly, until sugar is slightly browned. Pour a little of browned sugar from pan in each of 4 custard cups. Fill cups with milk mixture. Place cups in pan containing hot water and bake at 450° F. for 30 minutes, or until custard is well set and a pointed knife inserted in center comes out clean. Cool. Unmold on serving dish.

Serves 4.

WINE: Chilled Bordeaux Sauternes; chilled sweet Semillon.

OEUFS A LA NEIGE
(Floating Island)

Oeufs à la neige is an excellent and easy-to-make dessert. Served in an attractive bowl, it looks as good as it tastes.

A few pointers: Scald milk in a chicken fryer, because the high wall of a regular saucepan would make the poaching of the egg whites difficult. For shaping the beaten egg whites and dropping them in the milk, first dip spoon in warm water—this will prevent the egg whites from sticking to the spoon. Do not poach more than 4 spoonfuls at a time so that the egg whites will have room to expand and will not break.

2½ cups milk	3 eggs
⅓ cup granulated sugar	¼ teasp. salt
½ teasp. grated lemon	¼ cup powdered sugar
rind	1 teasp. cornstarch

Scald milk in a large pan. Add granulated sugar and lemon rind. Cover. Take pan off heat.

Separate eggs. Beat egg whites with salt until foamy, then gradually beat in powdered sugar, beating until

stiff. Return pan to heat and bring milk to boil. Lower
flame and keep at gentle simmer.

With kitchen spoon, lift spoonfuls of beaten egg whites
and drop them into milk. Cook for 1½ minutes. Turn
egg whites and cook other side for 2 minutes. Remove
eggs with perforated spoon and drain on dry cloth.

In top of double boiler, combine egg yolks with corn-
starch, gradually stirring in warm milk from pan. Place
over boiling water and cook, stirring constantly, for 5
minutes, or until mixture begins to thicken. Pour mixture into serving bowl. Chill. When ready to serve, float
the cooked egg whites on it.

Serves 4 to 6.

WINE: Chilled champagne; chilled Bordeaux Sauternes;
sweet Semillon.

DESSERT RICE

½ cup rice	½ teasp. salt
2 cups water	½-inch piece vanilla bean
2 cups milk	1 tablesp. butter
½ cup sugar	3 egg yolks, beaten

In large, heavy saucepan, place rice and water. Bring to
boil. Simmer for 5 minutes. Drain and rinse rice with
cold water. Return rice to pan. Add milk, sugar, salt, and
vanilla. Bring to boil. Add butter. Cover and simmer
over very low flame for 40 minutes. Let cool in the pan.
While still warm, stir in egg yolks. Gently press rice in
serving bowl.

WINE: Chilled Bordeaux Sauternes; chilled sweet Semillon.

RIZ AU LAIT
(Rice Custard)

Prepare dessert rice as above, but replace egg yolks
with whole eggs beaten until foamy.

Place rice mixture in a buttered ovenproof baking
dish. Sprinkle with 3 tablespoons granulated sugar. Place

under broiler flame for 5 minutes, or until sugar turns brown. Serve hot.

WINE: Chilled Bordeaux Sauternes; chilled sweet Semillon.

FRUITS CONDE

Prepare dessert rice as above. Warm canned halved fruits (peaches or pears) in own syrup. Drain. Place fruit on top of dessert rice. Cover with hot apricot sauce. Serve warm.

WINE: Chilled champagne; chilled Bordeaux Sauternes; sweet Semillon.

APRICOT SAUCE

1½ cups apricot jam	1 tablesp. sugar
½ cup water	2 tablesp. kirsh

In small, heavy saucepan, combine apricot jam, water, and sugar. Bring to boil and simmer for 5 minutes, stirring constantly. Add kirsh.

MARQUISE AU CHOCOLAT

4 squares semi-sweet chocolate	¼ lb. butter, cut into small pieces
2 tablesp. water	3 eggs, separated

In heavy saucepan, combine chocolate and water. Cook over low flame, stirring occasionally, until chocolate is well melted and smooth. Take pan off fire. Gradually stir in yolks, one at a time. Then stir in butter. Whip whites until stiff. Add whipped whites to chocolate mixture. Turn into well-buttered mold. Chill. Unmold. Serve covered with melted vanilla ice cream.

WINE: Chilled champagne

CREME PATISSIERE
(Bakers' Cream)

2 cups milk	⅓ cup flour
½ teasp. vanilla extract	pinch of salt
¾ cup sugar	6 egg yolks

Scald milk with vanilla. In heavy saucepan, combine sugar, flour, salt, and egg yolks. Stir until well blended. Add milk gradually. Cook over low flame, stirring constantly, being careful to scrape bottom of pan. Bring to boil and continue boiling for 3 minutes.

Pour cream in a bowl and let cool. Stir occasionally until cold.

WINE: Chilled Bordeaux Sauternes; chilled sweet Semillon.

PECHES MELBA

2 peaches	1 cup raspberries
4 tablesp. granulated	(fresh or frozen)
sugar	1 pint vanilla ice cream

⅛ cup slivered almonds

Poach peaches in boiling water. Let boil for 1 minute and remove to a bowl of ice water. Peel and halve peaches. Discard stones. Place peaches on dish and sprinkle with 2 tablespoons sugar. Let stand in refrigerator for ½ hour.

Meanwhile, rub raspberries through a sieve. Add remaining sugar. Mix well.

In individual dishes, place a layer of ice cream. Add half peach. Cover peach with raspberry mixture. Sprinkle with almonds.

Serves 4.

WINE: Chilled champagne

STRAWBERRY TIMBALE

4 cups strawberries	1 cup raspberries
(fresh or frozen)	(fresh or frozen)
⅛ cup granulated sugar	1 cup whipped cream

In a bowl, combine 3 cups strawberries and sugar. Let stand in refrigerator for 1 hour.

Through a sieve, rub remaining strawberries and raspberries. Combine with cream. Mix thoroughly but gently.

In sherbet glasses, place layer of strawberries from refrigerator. Cover with cream mixture. Serve chilled.
Serves 4.
WINE: Chilled champagne; chilled Bordeaux Sauternes;
sweet Semillon.

BANANA COUPE

4 bananas	4 tablesp. orange juice
2 tablesp. granulated sugar	2 tablesp. kirsch

Peel and cut bananas into slices ½ inch thick. Place
in shallow dish. Sprinkle with sugar. Add orange juice.
Let stand in refrigerator for ½ hour. Serve in sherbet
glasses. Sprinkle with kirsch.
Serves 4.
WINES: Chilled champagne; chilled Bordeaux Sauternes;
sweet Semillon.

BORDEAUX CHERRY COUPE

1 1-lb. can Bing cherries, drained	pinch of ground cinnamon
2 tablesp. granulated sugar	1 cup red Bordeaux wine

In saucepan, combine cherries, sugar, cinnamon, and
Bordeaux wine. Bring to boil. Simmer gently for 5 min-
utes. Chill. Serve in sherbet glasses.
Serves 4.
WINE: Chilled champagne; chilled Bordeaux Sauternes;
sweet Semillon.

ICED PEARS SAUTERNES

4 pears	2 tablesp. lemon juice
2 cups Sauternes wine	4 egg yolks
1¼ cups granulated sugar	1 pint vanilla ice cream

Peel pears and remove core.
In heavy saucepan, combine 1 cup wine and ¾ cup
sugar. Bring to boil and continue cooking for 5 minutes.
Add lemon juice and pears. Cook for 10 minutes. Chill
pears in cooking liquid.

Meanwhile, in small saucepan, heat remaining wine. Bring to boil and cook for 20 minutes, or until wine is reduced to approximately ½ cup.

Meanwhile, in top of double boiler, combine yolks and remaining sugar. Beat until creamy. Add reduced wine from pan. Cook, beating constantly, for 10 minutes, or until smooth and beginning to thicken.

In serving bowl, place layer of ice cream. Drain pears and arrange them on top of ice cream. Serve with wine sauce on the side.

Serves 4.

WINE: Chilled Bordeaux Sauternes; chilled sweet Semillon.

CHERRIES JUBILEE

Cherries jubilée is a spectacular dessert, invented by the great Escoffier in honor of Queen Victoria's Jubilee. Since then, it has remained a festive dessert that, like crêpes Suzette, is a source of attraction and delight.

For no good reason, it is not commonly made at home, although the recipe is so simple that the most inexperienced cook cannot but succeed in making it.

This is just the thing for the man of the house to show off his skill and to satisfy his deeply rooted dream of glory as a Chef "master of the fire."

After a full meal, it is a delicious, light dessert, and no trouble to prepare when you have expected, or unexpected, guests for dinner.

1 1-lb. can Bing cherries	2 tablesp. arrowroot,
2 tablesp. kirsch	dissolved in water

Drain cherries. Reserve juice from can.

In chafing dish or skillet, heat juice. Bring to boil and cook for 10 minutes. Add cherries. Bring again to boil. Add arrowroot and continue boiling for a few seconds, until liquid thickens. Sprinkle with slightly warmed kirsch and ignite. Serve quickly.

Serves 4.

WINE: Chilled champagne.

CHOCOLATE MOUSSE

⅛ cup strong coffee
  2 squares semi-sweet
    chocolate

3 teasp. sugar
4 egg yolks
5 egg whites

In small, heavy saucepan, combine coffee and chocolate. Heat until chocolate is melted, but do not allow to boil. Take pan off fire. Add sugar and stir until well blended. Stir in yolks one at a time. Turn into serving bowl. In mixing bowl, beat whites until firm. Fold beaten whites into chocolate mixture. Chill.

Serves 4 to 6.

BAKED APPLE

4 cooking apples
4 slices white bread

4 teasp. granulated sugar
4 teasp. butter

Peel and core apples. Cut slices of bread into circles about 2½ inches in diameter. Place bread in buttered baking dish. Place an apple on each piece of bread. In well in center of each apple, place 1 teasp. sugar. Add 1 teasp. butter on each apple. Bake at 375° F. for 30 minutes. Serve warm.

Serves 4.

WINE: Chilled Bordeaux Sauternes; chilled sweet Semillon.

Chapter XII

Very Special!

O N SOME very special occasions the thrifty French housewife throws caution overboard. Then she goes all the way; and afterward, if the family budget is limited, potatoes, macaroni, rice, beans, and lentils will recurrently appear on the table for a number of days.

Wealthy families are not so careful, and serve expensive dishes any time a pretext can be found for the lavishness of the meal.

After all, when you come down to essentials, the following dishes, for example, are only cheese canapés, noodles, potato salad.

One redeeming factor: they are superb.

CANAPE SANGRONIZ

1 1¼-oz. portion of Roquefort cheese	3 slices white bread
1 tablesp. butter	6 tablesp. Beluga caviar
1 teasp. sour cream	lemon juice

In mixing bowl, blend together Roquefort cheese, butter, and sour cream.

Toast bread. Spread toast with Roquefort cheese mixture. Top each canapé with 2 tablespoons caviar. Add a few drops of lemon juice. Cut each canapé into 4 equal strips.

Makes 12 canapés.

WINE: Chilled champagne.

NOUILLES MERILDA
(Noodles "Merilda")

Thus named because "Merilda," the family cook of Château Mouton-Rothschild, created it.

½ lb. noodles
2 lbs. coarsely chopped
mushrooms, cooked in
butter
3 large truffles, coarsely
chopped

1 egg yolk
1 teasp. salt
¼ teasp. pepper
¼ lb. grated Swiss cheese
butter

Cook noodles in boiling salted water. Drain. In mixing bowl, combine noodles, mushrooms, truffles, egg yolk, salt, and pepper. Mix well.

In ovenproof casserole, place one-third of noodles in a layer. Sprinkle with one-third of grated cheese. Repeat operation three times. Dot with butter. Bake at 350° F. for 20 minutes. Raise heat to 400° and continue baking for 10 minutes. Serve hot.

Serves 6.

WINE: *A chilled white wine:*
DRY: Bordeaux Graves; Alsatian Riesling or Traminer; Sauvignon Blanc.
SWEET: Bordeaux Sauternes; Gewurztraminer; sweet Semillon.

SALAD FRANCILLON

It is only a salad, but how delicious! It became popular in France (at least as popular as such an expensive dish can be) by the end of the nineteenth century.

The reason for its fame is that it was described in a play "Francillon" by Alexander Dumas Fils, the author of "La Dame aux Camelias" ("Camille").

It is not commonly made in France, but is made on special occasions—and it is a rare treat.

6 medium-size potatoes	2 tablesp. wine vinegar
2 cups consommé	½ cup Chateau Yquem, or
1½ teasp. salt	other first-class Bordeaux
¼ teasp. pepper	Sauternes wine
1 cup cooked and shelled	4 tablesp. olive oil
small mussels	1 tablesp. finely chopped
¼ teasp. tarragon	parsley
leaves (fresh or dried)	1 cup champagne

4 large truffles

In saucepan, combine potatoes, consommé, and 1 teaspoon salt. Bring to boil. Cover and simmer for 30 minutes, or until potatoes are well cooked. Drain. While still warm, peel potatoes and slice them. Place in salad bowl. Add mussels.

In mixing bowl, combine remaining salt, pepper, tarragon, vinegar, wine, oil, and parsley. Pour over potatoes and mussels. Toss gently but thoroughly.

Meanwhile, in small saucepan, combine champagne and truffles. Bring to boil. Cover and simmer for 10 minutes. Drain.

Cut truffles into slices and arrange on top of salad, covering the entire top with truffles. Let cool for 2 hours. (Do not put in refrigerator.)

Serves 6.

WINE: Chilled Bordeaux Sauternes; chilled sweet Semillon.

Chapter XIII

Non-Alcoholic Beverages

TEA

Tea is commonly drunk in France either at breakfast or after a meal, or more often at "tea-time," which is around 5:00 p.m.

It is prepared as in the United States and is also served in the same manner: plain, with lemon, or with milk.

COFFEE

French coffee is not as strong as the Italian "espresso" coffee, but is much stronger than American coffee.

Black Coffee

Black coffee is served after and between meals.

"Demi-tasse" simply means "half-cup." It is not a special way of making coffee. After meals, coffee is always served in France in small cups, different in size and style from teacups.

"Filtre" is coffee prepared and served in an individual

"filter" placed on the cup itself. It is generally finer than plain coffee, because it is made at the table and, therefore, is never reheated, and is always piping hot.

It is not possible to make French coffee with American-roasted coffee beans because most of the strength of the French brew comes from the fact that French coffee is roasted more. The coffee beans are really black and have a more bitter taste. French people grind coffee just before using it—which also contributes to its stronger flavor.

Contrary to what is commonly thought in this country, chicory is never added to black coffee by anyone who can afford not to use it. The only reason chicory is sometimes added to coffee is because it is cheaper, and the only time it is used by most people is in making café au lait for breakfast.

In most places in the United States, the closest one can get to French coffee is by combining half regular coffee with half of the Italian variety.

In the top of a drip coffee pot, place 1 tablespoon American-ground coffee and 1 tablespoon Italian-ground coffee per cup. Keep the pot warm.

Use 1 cup boiling water for each cup of coffee desired.

Pour 2 tablespoons boiling water over coffee and let stand for 5 minutes. Add remaining boiling water in small quantity (about 1/8 cup) at a time, being careful not to add new water as long as there is still water in top of pot.

Café au Lait

Café au lait (coffee with milk) is served at breakfast only.

Students, "bohemians," all classes of people with more leisure than money drink it at any odd time as a cheap and nourishing drink. They sit on the terrace of a café and for a few cents get a cup of café au lait—and the right to stay there for hours, discussing the most esoteric problems . . . or looking at the pretty girls passing by.

"Café au lait" is made by the addition of strong black coffee to a cup of hot milk.

CHOCOLATE

4 squares semi-sweet
   chocolate

4 cups boiling milk
2 egg yolks

In heavy saucepan, combine chocolate and ⅛ cup boiling milk. Keep warm, stirring until chocolate is melted. Take pan off fire. Add remaining boiling milk. Stir in yolks.* Add sugar to taste. Pour into chocolate pot.

With a whisk, beat chocolate in pot until foaming. Serve hot. Makes 4 cups.

HERB TEAS

Herb tea, or "tisane," as it is called in France, is liked by some and drunk by all.

Many healthy adults drink herb tea after meals, in lieu of coffee or tea, because they enjoy its delicate flavor. Children and older people who are forbidden coffee also drink it after meals. A cup of a carefully selected "tisane" is the first remedy to be forced on sick people. So, for one reason or another, every French person, man, woman or child, has gallons of "tisane" in his past, present, and future.

Each herb is credited with its own medicinal virtues. They are the "remède de bonne femme" (old woman's remedy) par excellence. However, physicians sometimes prescribe them and there is perhaps something to be said for the age-old belief in herbs.

Antique lovers know the lovely pots, standing on a candle-warmer, which were used to keep warm "tisane" at the convalescent's bedside. During the day, herb tea is prepared and served in a regular teapot reserved for this use.

For making herb tea, place 1 teaspoon of dried leaves (or flowers) per cup in warmed teapot. Pour boiling water over herb. Cover and let stand for 5 minutes before serving. If you prefer a stronger infusion, use more of the herb.

ANISE—Very fragrant. Supposed to relieve abdominal pains.

* See "How to blend with egg yolks" on page 125.

BERGAMOT—Drunk for the exquisite flavor only.

BORAGE (dried flowers)—Borage infusion is widely used for chest pains. Not much can be said for the flavor itself.

CAMOMILLE (dried flowers)—This is one of the stars of the herb kingdom. It has a lovely pale gold color and a delicate fragrance. It is fresh and soothing, and is a pleasant after-meal drink. It is recommended as a "tranquillizer." As such, a cup of strongly sweetened camomille is taken at bedtime by people suffering from insomnia or nervousness.

Many a Frenchwoman occasionally uses cooking ingredients as simple and "natural" cosmetics: egg yolks are used as a skin nourishment; whipped egg whites, as an astringent; cucumber juice, crushed strawberries, to freshen the skin. The list of "nature's cosmetics" to be found in the kitchen is a long one. Camomille is one that is supposed to have as much value for "external use" as for "internal" one.

Brushing the face with camomille and soap is supposed to keep the skin smooth, supple, and young. Rinsing blond hair with a strong infusion of camomille is said to give it a lovely sparkle.

No French housewife would be caught without a good supply of camomille.

LINDEN (dried or fresh leaves)—Has a very fine flavor. Like camomille, it is considered to be soothing, and is recommended against insomnia and nervousness.

MINT (fresh or dried leaves)—Mint has a well-known wonderfully fresh flavor. It is served as a stimulant to digestion and as a tonic. And, of course, a few fresh mint leaves added to iced tea makes one of the coolest hot-weather drinks.

PARSLEY—Supposed to relieve abdominal pains. French "créoles" used to bath their face with cold parsley infusion to protect their complexion against suntan. Whether it helps, nobody knows, because nowadays nobody wishes to avoid suntan.

VERBENA—Delightfully perfumed and of an exquisite taste. It is recommended in cases of stomach upset.

Index

179

SOUP'S ON!

☐ **THE TUESDAY SOUL FOOD COOKBOOK.** 200 easy-to-use recipes from *Tuesday Magazine*—with everything from black-eyed peas to pig's knuckles—in the first soul food cookbook in paperback.
(PE4708—$1.00)

☐ **AMERICA'S FAVORITE RECIPES FROM BETTER HOMES & GARDENS.** From appetizers to luscious desserts—over 500 prize-tested recipes—275 photographs!
(NE4578—95¢)

☐ **HAWAII COOKBOOK & BACKYARD LUAU** by Elizabeth Ahn Toupin. 175 succulent recipes plus tempting menu suggestions to turn your kitchen into an exotic tropical paradise!
(SE13—75¢)

☐ **James Beard's HORS D'OEUVRES & CANAPES.** Great for party-giving success—sizzling taste treats and cool bite-size delights.
(SE4384—75¢)

☐ **THE ART OF BARBECUE COOKING.** What to cook on—what to cook with—full-color photographs of many appetizing dishes—plus a special chapter on sauces.
(NE4782—95¢)

☐ **THE FANNIE FARMER JUNIOR COOKBOOK** by Wilma Lord Perkins. The famous, illustrated guide that's been the favorite of young cooks for over two decades.
(SE4677—75¢)

☐ **THE COMPLETE BOOK OF MEXICAN COOKING** by Elisabeth Ortiz. 340 delicious recipes in the most complete and colorful guide to Mexican cooking ever written.
(NE4107—95¢)

☐ **THE SPANISH COOKBOOK** by Barbara Norman. Precise and simple directions for over 200 of the best recipes from the kitchens of Spain.
(SE4389—75¢)

☐ **AN HERB AND SPICE COOKBOOK** by Craig Clairborne. The food editor of *The New York Times* presents over 400 original and tempting recipes, prepared with dozens of different herbs and spices—a subtle choice of the finest cuisines throughout the world.
(SE4077—75¢)

Ask for them at your local bookseller or use this handy coupon: